Kama Sutra

For 21st-Century Lovers

Kama Sutra

For 21st-Century Lovers

Anne Hooper

LONDON, NEW YORK, MUNICH,
MELBOURNE, DELHI

Brand manager: Lynne Brown
Senior editor: Salima Hirani
Project editor: Susannah Steel
Art director: Carole Ash
**Designer and photographic
art director:** Toni Kay
Photographer: Russel Kientsch
DTP designer: Karen Constanti
Production controller: Sarah Sherlock
Jacket editor: Beth Apple
Jacket designer: Nicola Powling
Category publisher: Corinne Roberts

The more athletic positions in this
book may prove to be too dangerous
for some readers. Please do not attempt
these positions if you suffer from any kind
of physical pain or restricted movement,
or if you are physically unfit.

First American Edition, 2003

Published in the United States by
DK Publishing, Inc.
375 Hudson Street
New York, New York 10014

03 04 05 06 07 08 10 9 8 7 6 5 4 3 2 1

Library of Congress Cataloging-in-Publication Data
Hooper, Anne, 1941-
    Kama Sutra for 21st-century lovers / Anne Hooper
  p. cm.
Includes index.
    ISBN 0-7894-9655-0 (alk. paper)
1. Sex. 2. Love. 3. Sexual intercourse. I. Title: Kama
Sutra for twenty-first-century lovers. II. Title.
    HQ31.H7444 2003
    613.9'6 - - dc21   2003053064

Reproduced by GRB, Italy
Printed and bound in Hong Kong by
Toppan Printing Co. (HK) Ltd.

Discover more at
www.dk.com

Contents

Introduction

This book is the fifth version of the *Kama Sutra* that my publishers have asked me to write. It's an extraordinary fact, but the four versions that came before have so gripped the imagination of lovers worldwide that my readers are eager to learn even more. I've heard that previous editions have been given as engagement or wedding presents, and that parents unashamedly pick up copies from the coffee tables of their grown-up children and browse through them. Pocket versions of the book have been slipped under pillows, into Christmas stockings, or delicately wrapped and given as Valentine's Day gifts. So what is it about this particular book that so intrigues?

The answer has to lie in the fascinating mix of exotic sensual experiences and lavishly illustrated images that encompass both the ancient and modern worlds. There is something timeless and enduring about this and the other classic Eastern sex manuals, giving them a prestige more modern sex books do not possess. This produces a heady mix when combined with the dazzling yet sensitive photographs of loving couples that illustrate these famous sex positions without offense. Ultimately, this book aims to satisfy our curiosity about one of the most profound aspects of our existence—human sexuality.

The story of the Kama Sutra

At some time between the 1st and 4th centuries AD, *a Brahman called Vatsyayana collated a series of ancient Sanskrit writings on the art of love and sexual technique. Brahmans were Indian noblemen and scholars who believed that life consisted of* dharma, artha, *and* kama. Dharma *was the acquisition of religious merit,* artha *was the acquisition of wealth and* kama *was the acquisition of love or sensual pleasure.*

Vatsyayana's intention was that the *Kama Sutra* would help his fellow noblemen develop that third tenet of life, *kama,* by helping them to get the very best out of sensual experiences, on the grounds that the more profound a loving encounter becomes, the more *kama* your spirit gains. Vatsyayana laid down practical guidelines to ensure success in such a life ambition. For example, he knew that the more beauty you fill the senses with, the greater the individual's potential for gaining ecstatic orgasm becomes. And in the *Kama Sutra* the ecstasy of orgasm, at its very best, is considered to be a type of nirvana, a mini-heaven.

The words *"kama sutra"* may bring to mind hundreds of extraordinary sex poses, yet Vatsyayana listed only eight basic positions. These were first described by an earlier author, Babhravya, while variations on these positions were actually written by another early writer, Suvarnanabha. (We illustrate those eight positions, and their variations, in Chapter Two.)

The book was aimed at men, since women at that time were considered inferior and subservient to their men. Interestingly, the *Kama Sutra* does not neglect women. There are many pages detailing how male lovers can excite female sensuality, including types of kisses and touches, plus sexual positions that women initiate. For example, Vatsyayana includes three woman-on-top forms of lovemaking to be used when the woman "acts the part of the man." He recommends that if a woman "sees her lover is fatigued by constant

This ritual Yoni vessel represents the female sexual organs as well as the divine feminine energy.

congress, without having his desire satisfied, she would, with his permission, lay him down upon his back and give him assistance by acting his part. She may also do this to satisfy the curiosity of her lover, or her own desire of novelty."

Vatsyayana also advocated specific positions to suit a couple's sexual requirements. A high congress position, such as Wife of Indra *(p.34)*, enables a man with a small penis to achieve maximum penetration with a lover who has a deep vagina. Low congress, such as the Twining Position *(p.42)*, allows a man with a large penis to penetrate a woman with a small vagina.

The Western world first came to hear of the *Kama Sutra* through the enthusiasm of the famous Victorian explorer Richard Burton. Burton and his colleague, Forster Fitzgerald Arbuthnot, brought the manuscript to England, translated it and then published it in 1883. This was an extraordinarily daring thing to do at the time, since Victorian society decidedly did not approve. In order to avoid prosecution for obscenity, Burton formed the Kama Shastra Society, which allowed subscribers to purchase the book privately. In this way Burton escaped the heavy hand of the law, yet nevertheless became infamous for his publication. The eloquent language of the Victorian translation gives the book a unique flavor.

The lingam represents the divine male principle, the creative energy of the god Shiva, the creator and destroyer.

The Ananga Ranga

Two years after the publication of the Kama Sutra, *Burton and Arbuthnot published the* Ananga Ranga, *another ancient sex manual from the East. "Ananga Ranga" means "Stage of the Bodiless One," which refers to the moment when the Hindu god of love, Kama, became a bodiless spirit while his physical body was burned to a pile of ashes by a stare from the third eye of the great god Shiva.*

The ancient writings teach that sexuality is as important as acquiring power or offering prayers to the gods.

The *Ananga Ranga* shares similarities with the *Kama Sutra*, since both draw on the same ancient scripts. They differ in the fact that they were written a few centuries apart—the *Ananga Ranga* was compiled as an individual title, for it was written sometime around AD 1172.

By the time the *Ananga Ranga* first appeared, Indian society had become more ordered than in Vatsyayana's time and extramarital sex was now censured.

While the *Kama Sutra* was written for lovers, married or otherwise, the author of *Ananga Ranga*, Kalyana Malla, explained that his motive was to protect marriage from the sexual tedium that he thought could easily set in: "The chief reason for the separation between the married couple, and the cause which drives the husband to the embraces of strange women, and the wife to the arms of strange men, is the want of varied pleasures, and the monotony which follows possession."

The *Ananga Ranga* was written shortly before the start of the Crusades, which, despite the bloodshed, was a time of great cultural exchange between East and West. Returning European crusaders brought back with them Eastern erotic refinements such as cleanliness and sexual foreplay. A few centuries later, the text was discovered by Burton and Arbuthnot and added to their Victorian list of classic Eastern literary erotica.

The Perfumed Garden

The third book that Richard Burton obtained, translated and published under the auspices of his Kama Shastra Society initially surfaced in the mid-1800s in Algeria, having been bought by a French officer who was stationed there.

The Perfumed Garden was written by Sheikh Nefzawi, who is believed to have lived in Tunisia during the 16th century. Like the *Kama Sutra*, *The Perfumed Garden* includes much more than sexual positions: sensual foods, aphrodisiacs, and sexually desirable partners are all explored and discussed.

Sheikh Nefzawi was clearly an experienced and wise man in sexual matters, and while *The Perfumed Garden* is mainly concerned with giving advice to men, it also keeps the sexual welfare of women clearly in mind. In the male-dominated culture of North Africa of that time, this was enlightened subject matter.

The Sheikh believed that men who deserved to succeed with women were those who were "anxious to please them." In his opinion, the ideal male possessed "a member that grows, gets strong, vigorous and hard" when close to a woman. "His member should be able to reach the end of the canal of the female and completely fill it in all its parts." In other words, the Sheikh believed that biggest was best—a hotly debated issue in the 21st century. Meanwhile, a woman, in Nefzawi's view, needed "the lower part of the belly to be large, the vulva projecting and fleshy," and "the conduit to be narrow and not moist, soft to the touch and emitting a strong heat." The "not moist" reference emphasizes one of the differences between Eastern and Western culture that continues today. Arabic women prefer to remain "dry," since they believe it makes intercourse sexier.

A 19th-century erotic painting from the Chinese School.

The Tao

The last chapter in this book focuses on The Tao, *a collection of ancient Chinese wisdom that predates the other writings. Taoism is a system of philosophical belief. At its heart is the belief that ultimate harmony exists in the universe, and this can be attained by following the Tao. The word "Tao" means "path," but in Taoism it also signifies the functioning of the universe.*

Unlike the rather austere philosophies of the present era, sexuality played an active part in ancient Chinese Taoist philosophy. Taoists believe that life is a balance of opposites in which everything that occurs has an equal and opposite reaction. Animating all that exists in the entire universe are twin forces: Yin, which is negative, passive, and nourishing; and Yang, which is positive, active, and consuming. The major component of a woman's nature is seen as Yin, while a man is predominantly Yang. An imbalance of Yin and Yang exists between the sexes, so that a woman needs the male force and a man needs the female force to achieve balance. These forces are exchanged by sexual union, and it is at orgasm that they are at their most potent.

Taoist thinkers advocate that sexual stimulation should be protracted in order to reach the highest levels of arousal. This is not just for sensual pleasure; its main purpose is to promote sexual health and energy. The Tao of Sex is one of eight pillars of Taoist wisdom, and Taoist sexology aims to improve health, harmonize relationships, and increase spiritual realization *(see also p.123)*. Thus the correct application of Taoist sex techniques is to restore the body's energy, and the ultimate Taoist aim is to prolong life itself—the logical result of this being immortality.

In this context, the ancient Chinese perceived lovemaking as an art form, and some of the names of the positions are wonderfully artistic—the Galloping Horse, Butterflies in Flight, Swallows in Love, and Silkworm Spinning a Cocoon are all intensely visual, evocative descriptions.

The *Kama Sutra* teaches that sensual and sexual pleasures delight the senses and revive the spirit.

FOR THE READER

My aim in this edition of the *Kama Sutra* is to offer readers a 21st-century slant on the sexual advice contained in these ancient writings. These days, it seems to be women who buy books about sex (mainly to give to their men, I suspect), so I have adapted this volume to contain advice for both men and women.

There are also some essential points to remember to get the best out of your lovemaking. The *Kama Sutra* makes absolutely clear the importance of comfort and aesthetics in your allotted room for love, which should be "balmy with rich perfumes… a bed, soft and agreeable to the sight, covered with a white cloth, low in the middle part, having garlands and flowers upon it.…" Cleaning the body, relaxing the mind, dimming the lights, and playing sensual music all figure in the love plan. Since Vatsyayana's excellent advice is here being projected onto the 21st century, I would suggest the addition of a glass or two of champagne, a light meal, the gift of playful massage, and oceans of unhurried time. Unfortunately, the 20th century speeded up the lovemaking experience, thanks to the convenience of the contraceptive pill and the demands of everyday stress. But Vatsyayana knew that the best love ingredients of all are to be non-pressuring, non-demanding, and simply sensual—much better aims for this new century.

While I have included, wherever possible, the Victorian translators' eloquent language to retain a touch of its unique flavor, my commentary brings a modern perspective to these ancient sex positions that lovers today can relate to. This sometimes includes a certain irreverence on my part when, for example, I mention that a particular sexual position can be enjoyed only by the most supple of acrobats! And the humor inherent in many of the original descriptions of sex positions is irresistible. You might find that Kama's Wheel may not do a lot for your orgasms, but you'll have fabulous fun performing it!

I hope that, as well as learning skillful techniques, readers will be reminded of the fact that sex can be spiritually uplifting. If you believe this, I hope you will welcome the idea of using loving sex as a gateway to spirituality. Ultimately, I hope that you, the reader, will gain new insights into your own character and behavior by browsing through this book and picking up some wonderful practical tips to enable you to make amazing love to your adored partner. With any luck, you will feel some of his/her gain, too.

Anne J. Hooper

Preparing for love

Erogenous zones

Skin—the largest organ—covers the entire body in nerve endings. When sensitive areas are stroked, these nerve endings get stimulated and pockets of explosive sensation erupt. These touch-sensitive areas are known as erogenous zones.

The breasts

for her

The author of the *Kama Sutra*, Vatsyayana, gave good advice to male lovers eager to explore their partner's erogenous zones: "He should always make a point of pressing those parts of her body on which she turns her eyes." This makes sense when you realize that not every woman gains erotic feeling from breast and nipple sensation. Thus the man should take his cue from the woman's reaction (or lack of it) when softly stroking her breasts.

for him

What Vatsyayana did not say in the *Kama Sutra* was that many men also feel fantastic sensations from breast and nipple play.

If your nipples react to being kissed, sucked, and licked by your partner, they quickly become very sensual and exciting points of stimulus for you. You may enjoy having your breasts squeezed and massaged gently instead. If you don't feel very much when you are stroked directly on the breasts or nipples, ask your lover to try stroking the sides of your breasts delicately, which can sometimes invoke more sensations.

Let your woman run her fingers softly around your nipples and then brush her fingertips from side to side across the top so that her fingers actually leave the nipples before going back in the opposite direction. You may be excited by the way your body reacts to these sensations, and even more so if your woman begins these actions slowly and then speeds up.

Ears

Nape of neck

Back

Mouth

Hands

The buttocks

For both sexes, the buttocks can awaken primitive sexual urges in our brains—an instinct we share with our "cousins" the apes. Women tend to find men's buttocks sexier than the penis, and men have been known to be turned on by simply looking at a woman's buttocks. Small wonder that touching, caressing, and stroking your lover in this area can give such pleasure, not just to your partner, but also to yourself.

for him

Your woman need not be afraid of touching you firmly; some men have such powerful musculature that their buttocks feel quite hard when handled. She might try moving your buttocks in circles underneath the flat of her hand, which will make you feel pleasantly manipulated. If you want a stronger sensation, tell her it is fine if she moves more of your body than your buttock muscles with her hands.

for her

Being stroked on your buttocks softly can feel deeply sensual and erotic. So, too, can your man's spanking you lightly with the flat of his hand. A little gentle spanking that stings very slightly arouses the blood and makes the body tingle. Your man could bear in mind that it's also an exciting turn-on when it comes as a surprise, as long as it is done gently.

*Inside
elbow*

Inside thigh

*Underside
of knee*

The feet

The extraordinary fact about foot massage is that it provokes incredible sensations over the body, especially in the sensitive inner thigh area.

for him

The ball of each foot should be kneaded to penetrate the outer layers of skin. Strong finger manipulation across the area under your toes provokes powerful prickles of sensuality. Your partner can run a lubricated finger sensuously between each of your toes to transmit sensations directly to your genitals.

for her

Ask your lover to hold the heel of your foot in one hand and gently grasp the toes with the other hand, then slowly rotate your foot in the fullest circle possible. This triggers sensual nerves in the inner thighs.

Grooming and massage

Many lovers play slippery sex games in the shower, but everyday actions such as bathing and shampooing can be more than just fun. Grooming each other in preparation for lovemaking can be tender yet charged with eroticism as you rediscover one another's bodies, while a well-performed massage is no less than a sexual experience in itself.

Bathing together

Floating in a warm bath soothes and stabilizes certain vital organs and helps you feel relaxed, so taking a bath with your lover is a perfect preliminary to lovemaking. The attention you give each other's bodies lulls you both into a deepening sense of security and intimacy.

for him

You may enjoy the thrill of feeling like a naughty little boy again as your woman soaps your body. Your excitement can only increase as she stretches down into the water and explores those intimate parts of your body that may be harder to reach.

for her

Relax and let your partner devote his attentions to exploring your wet body with his hands and eyes. By soaping you and rubbing you delicately all over, he can make your skin tingle and subtly arouse you both mentally and physically.

Buttocks

Strong massage strokes can stimulate the buttocks, so relax them first with deep kneading. Make sure there is enough massage oil on your hands so they slip smoothly across the surface of your lover's skin.

for him
After the initial deep strokes, your partner can glide her hands from the top of your thighs over your buttocks, leaning her body weight into the strokes. You should experience this as a rush of sensation, especially if her strokes are tantalizingly slow.

for her
Your partner can try firm circling strokes, then light strokes with the whole hand, fingertip strokes, and finally he can use his fingernails to scratch your skin softly. This can feel sensational.

Feet and legs

For massage oil, the 4th-century readers of the *Kama Sutra* would have used a natural oil such as almond or coconut, perfumed with essence of rose, jasmine, patchouli, ylang-ylang, or sandalwood. You might add a dozen drops of one of these to 2 tablespoons (30 ml) of the base oil. Start by massaging the toes. Stretch, knead, and bend each one, then rub between them. Stroke along the foot and up the leg. Stretch the leg by bending it at the knee before moving on to the inner thigh.

for him
The fragranced oil and the feel of your partner's warm hands are deeply relaxing. The higher her hands travel up your legs, the more you will become aroused as your body and mind concentrate on her repetitive stroking patterns.

for her
Your lover can use his thumbs to cover your feet with tiny circles—a highly sensuous stroke. He can excite you further by kissing each of the circles he has created.

Favorite massage strokes

Circling Use your palms in a circular motion, either large or small, on your partner's body.
Fingertips Continue the circling movement, but use the fingertips.
Sexual strokes Use your fingernails instead of your fingertips for these light strokes (called feathering) on your partner's hot spots.

Using massage oil

You don't need to use a massage oil, but your strokes will be smooth and erotic if your hands are coated with a sweet-smelling oil. Either buy a prepared massage oil or make up your own *(see p.15)*. The visual and sensual appeal of shiny, slippery skin can be immensely arousing.

"... apply a limited quantity of ointments, perfume to the body, eat betel leaves that give fragrance to the mouth, bathe daily, anoint your body with oil every other day and remove the sweat of the armpits."

Back and spine

The golden rule of back massage is to place your hands on either side of the spine, but never directly on it. Begin by covering the back with circular strokes, moving away from the spine. This helps to smooth away the pressures of the day so you can start your lovemaking in a relaxed state of mind. Keep your strokes slow and sexy.

for him

Some men hold a lot of tension in their muscles, so their skin feels particularly taut. For massage to make any real impression on an "armored" male, he needs deep pressure. Ask your woman to put her entire body weight behind her strokes to ease your stiff muscles. But not all men hold such tension in their bodies and may prefer lighter strokes. Ask your woman to use the type of stroke that will relieve your tension best.

for her

If you are thin and delicately boned, you'll have very little flesh that your man's strong hands can manipulate, so ensure that his strokes are not too strong and forceful, or you may end up being bruised rather than pleasured. Your partner should make use of light palm-skimming and fingertip treatment to make your skin tingle and feel alive.

Arms and torso

Use a light circling stroke across the chest. Starting at the shoulders, stroke down along the torso. Move the breasts in circles, then trace your fingertips around the breasts and nipples. When you reach the stomach and pelvis, move your hands to the thighs and circle them slowly toward the pubic area. Then work up across the abdomen and ribs and end by massaging the breasts and shoulders once more. To massage an arm, wrap your hands around it and pull them, one hand after the other, down along the arm several times.

for him

Women are often unaware that many men possess extremely responsive nipples. A chest massage is the perfect time to discover how sensitive yours may be. Your partner can bring added eroticism to the massage by applying gentle pressure around your groin area.

for her

Ensure that your lover's hands are well coated with oil so they slip across your responsive skin. Light strokes feel most enticing and erotic. Many women enjoy breast massage immensely, but don't focus on this alone. Nerve endings in the arms and hands can be enlivened by touch and send out erotic feelings to the entire torso.

Shoulders and head

Massage the neck and shoulders first, offering a light thumb and forefinger massage to move the flesh across and around the powerful neck muscles that hold up the head. Then, using thumb and fingertips, move up into the hairline and work your way across the top of the head.

for her

After the preliminary head massage, your man can use light thumb-circling on your temples, then cover your forehead with tiny fingertip circles. Such delicate strokes help you to relax and focus on touch. He can use his forefingers to circle across your cheeks (avoiding the eye area) and down under your chin, then stroke his hands along your neck and back to your breasts to arouse you.

for him

For many men, the head and shoulder massage not only affects the immediate site of the massage, but also sends out prickles of pleasure across the rest of the body. It can be very pleasurable if your partner shampoos your hair as she massages, working into the roots of your hair and scalp.

Kissing

Kissing stimulates the senses of touch, taste, and smell and inspires strong emotions. The author of the *Kama Sutra*, Vatsyayana, recognized kissing as an art form and described in detail a variety of kisses for different occasions, be it a light, almost casual brushing of lips or a deep, penetrating experience in which a couple remains locked in a long embrace.

The bent kiss

Place your hand around your partner's neck to guide their mouth toward yours. This is a natural and gentle preliminary kiss in which the lovers' faces are angled easily and comfortably toward each other.

for him

For a kiss to work well, it needs to be light enough to allow for lip movement. Your woman may like to pucker her lips, then relax them. Such movement signifies her erotic response to you and will begin to stoke the fires of your passion.

for her

Your lover could turn your face to one side as he kisses you (so his cheek presses on yours), then turn it back (so his lips roll back onto yours). This sensual move gives a feeling of intimacy.

The turned kiss

This kiss should be performed by the tallest partner, usually the man. Hold your lover's chin and turn her face up to meet your kiss. Use this kiss to initiate sex or while making love slowly in a face-to-face position.

for her

If, like many women, you find this move very sexy, your passion will be fired by this romantic, tactile gesture. If you are panicked by such manipulation, place your hand on his chest as a barrier to show him he should move on to something else.

for him

Kiss your lover gently and try to tune in to her response. If she throws her arms around you, you know you have gotten it right and you can kiss with more passion and urgency.

The straight kiss

For this kiss, your faces are level rather than angled to one side, so tongue penetration is impractical. This is a gentle way to show affection and express desire.

for him and her

Don't be afraid of staying with this kiss for a while. It offers you time in which to feel comfortable with intimacy before moving on to something deeper. If it feels natural, take such innocent kisses further into a more sexual and erotic exchange.

The pressed kiss

This kiss, not often used in the West, is perhaps one we should experiment with a little more. One lover holds the other's lower lip, touches it with their tongue, and then kisses it "with great force."

for him

This highly erotic and intense exercise can be used as a prelude to deep kissing—a kind of "playing with the lips." Look into your lover's eyes as you press her lower lip, to increase her passion and signal the release of your own suppressed desires.

for her

This kiss is light enough to withdraw from, should that be your immediate instinct, without causing damage to the relationship. This security can be helpful when getting to know a new lover.

Kissing the body

The lips are sensitive to kissing, but so are other sites on the body, especially those close to the genitals. Vatsyayana says that "kissing is of four kinds: moderate, contracted, pressed and soft, according to the different parts of the body which are kissed, for different kinds of kisses are appropriate for different parts of the body."

Kiss definition

Moderate kisses These are measured, without too much intensity, such as a tender kiss on the back or a smooching progression up along the spine.

Contracted kisses Little staccato kisses are used in this technique in which you apply your lips to the skin, then quickly pull away in a playful, affectionate manner. You might lavish these on your partner's buttocks or thighs.

Pressed kisses Apply gentle pressure while holding your mouth on your partner's body for a moment. Make it feel as if you are almost reluctant to withdraw your lips.

Soft kisses The most tender, gentle kiss, with which you just brush your partner's skin, is the soft kiss. Lavish these on sensitive areas such as the neck and throat, moving down toward the chest.

Breast kissing

Apply kisses lightly to the swell of each breast and, if the mood takes you, turn your kisses into gentle sucking or nibbling. Don't be afraid to pay a lot of attention to the nipples and the sides of the breasts. Stimulate your partner's genitals while kissing this area for maximum impact.

for him

Some men find their breasts only become sensitive once their genitals are stimulated. Others have the opposite experience. Take no chances and ask for both areas to be caressed as your woman snuggles up to you.

for her

You will enjoy your man gently licking or biting his way from your sensitive abdomen to your breasts. His fingers can caress the lower side of your breasts while his mouth covers the top and nipples with tiny kisses.

Kissing and licking

Tongue bathing only works well when performed on a hot, balmy evening or in an unusually warm room since once your body is damp, it begins to feel the cold quickly. However, kissing and licking your way up and down your partner's body can be an extremely sensual experience for you both.

for him and her

Pay special attention to those sensitive areas such as the breasts and nipples, the insides of the thighs, and the backs of the knees to heighten the sense of anticipation. The greater the self-control you practice as you delay penetration with this artful foreplay, the richer the rewards when it does happen.

Kama Sutra kisses

Among the *Kama Sutra*'s many descriptions of kissing are:
• The demonstrative kiss, given when "at night, at a theater, or in an assembly of caste men, a man coming up to a woman kisses a finger of her hand if she be standing, or a toe of her foot if she be sitting, or when a woman is shampooing her lover's body, places her face on his thigh (as if she were sleepy) so as to inflame his passion, and kisses his thigh or great toe."
• The transferred kiss, which is when a person "kisses a child sitting on his lap, or a picture, or an image, or figure, in the presence of the person beloved by him."
• The kiss showing intention, when a person "kisses the reflection of the person he loves in a mirror, in water or on a wall."

Cunnilingus

The *Kama Sutra* does not appear to consider cunnilingus a particularly interesting activity since there is only one brief reference to it in the original manuscript. In the 21st century, however, cunnilingus constitutes a valuable—and, for some, essential—element of a satisfactory sexual experience.

Using cunnilingus

The natural state of the vagina, when stimulated, is to become lubricated, which then spontaneously facilitates penetration. It also triggers sexual sensations in a woman. Try lovemaking without this natural lubrication and it immediately becomes obvious that the experience is a painful and distinctly unerotic one for the woman. Human saliva is close to the consistency of natural vaginal fluid, and if the woman's vaginal lips are coated with saliva, it will immediately encourage her arousal.

There are different techniques a man can use to vary the sensations his woman feels *(see right)*. Your woman may prefer some over others. Use her responses to guide you as you perfect these techniques and develop some more of your own.

Licking up the labia
Pass the broad blade of your tongue along and between the labia majora (large lips). Run your tongue up and down these crevices several times.

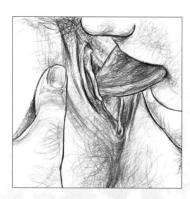

Penetrating strokes
Using first shallow strokes and then deeper and deeper ones, move the tip of your tongue up and down inside the opening of her vagina, as well as in and out of it.

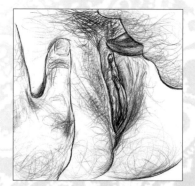

Licking the clitoris
With the tip of your tongue, coat the clitoris with moisture by licking upward only. Try licking up one side of the clitoris and then the other rather than directly on it. Many women find there is more sensation on the left side.

Twirling on the clitoris head
Using the tip of your tongue, circle the top of the clitoris very lightly. Try this in a clockwise then a counterclockwise motion. Some women are extremely sensitive and find that this action blunts their sensation, so be prepared to experiment.

Clitoral stimulation

The clitoris is probably the most sensitive nerve center of a woman's body. For cunnilingus to work well, you should position yourself between your woman's legs so you can cover her clitoris and genital lips with the broad blade of your tongue. Stroke your tongue upward over the shaft and head of the clitoris, then stimulate each side of the clitoris in turn, always working from the base to the top. Using featherlike strokes on the head of the clitoris and flicking the underside from side to side with the tip of your tongue will give your woman maximum pleasure and help her to climax.

"A man should always make a point of pressing those parts of a woman's body on which she turns her eyes."

Kama Sutra

Fellatio

In the *Kama Sutra*, Vatsyayana defines *auparishtaka*, or "mouth congress," as an activity predominantly practiced by eunuchs on their masters. He describes how "eunuchs disguised as males keep their desires secret and when they wish to do anything they lead the life of a shampooer." Vatsyayana goes on to explain that under the pretense of shampooing (washing and massaging the body), the eunuch fondles and excites his master, eventually pleasuring him with eight kinds of fellatio, one after the other. In the 21st century, fellatio is practiced by many heterosexual couples and is considered an enticing addition to a woman's repertoire of lovemaking skills.

Licking the penis

The woman starts fellatio by licking her man's penis as if it were an ice-cream cone. She holds the base of the penis in one hand and, using the blade of her tongue, repeatedly licks upward, first on one side and then on the other.

21st–century technique

The "butterfly flick" is an up-to-date addition to fellatio techniques. The woman holds her man's penis steady with one hand while she flicks her tongue lightly from side to side along the ridge on the underside of his penis.

The eight kinds of fellatio

Vatsyayana's eunuchs turned fellatio into a game. Every time they finished performing one of these eight variations, they would stop and wait until their master asked for more before continuing on to the next technique.

The nominal congress
Place the head of the penis between your lips and move it around.

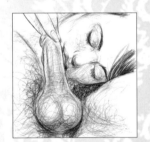

Biting the sides
Gently nibble on the shaft of the penis.

Pressing outside
Press the end of the penis gently with your lips and draw it out.

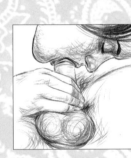

Pressing inside
Put the end of the penis into your mouth before pressing it with your lips and withdrawing.

Kissing the penis
Kiss the penis while holding it in your hand.

Rubbing the penis
Touch the penis all over with your tongue and mouth.

Sucking a mango fruit
Insert half of the penis into your mouth and suck it.

Swallowing up the penis
Put the whole penis into your mouth as if you are about to swallow it.

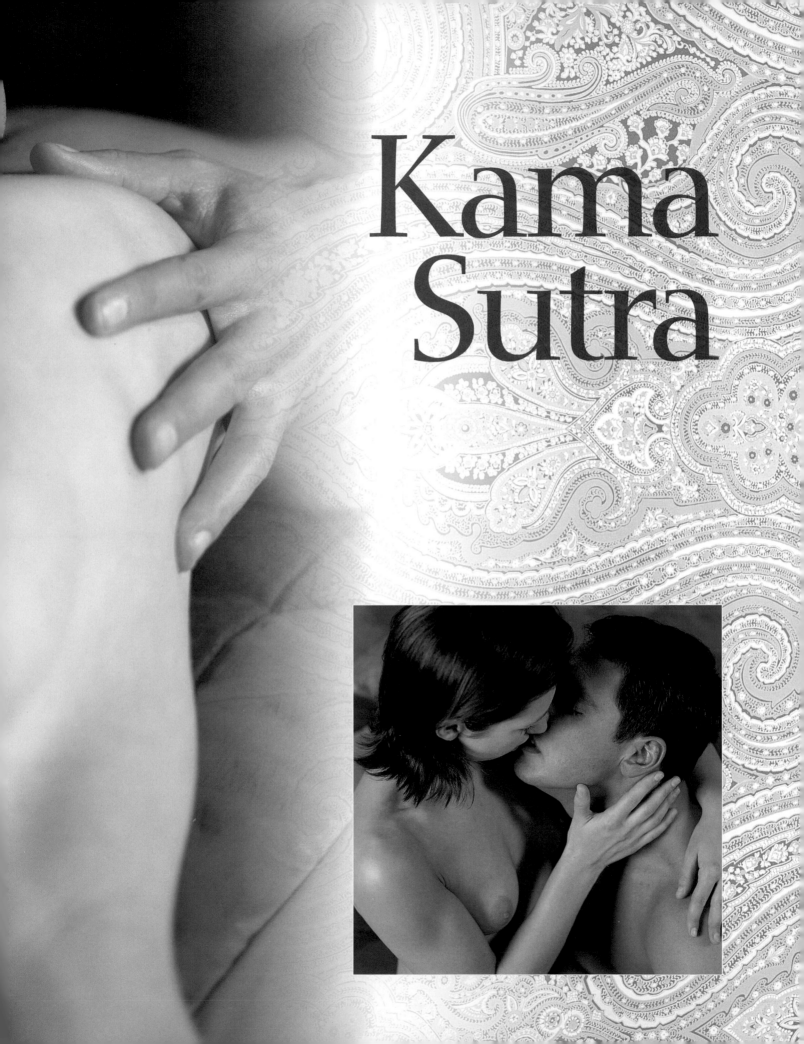

Kama Sutra

Stimulating the clitoris

The author of the Kama Sutra described man-on-top positions in which the woman's legs are open wide, allowing the man to move in close. He never mentions the clitoris, but is certain to have known how it functions; these positions allow for maximum clitoral stimulation by the man's penis and abdomen.

WIDELY OPENED POSITION

In this position, in which the woman arches her back so that her pelvis moves up to join the man, she can make it very clear how eager she is for penetration.

for her ★★★★☆

As you lean back on your elbows, you will gain the perfect opportunity to gaze into your lover's face and watch his excitement. Face-to-face positions like this can be emotionally arousing, although this one is extremely tiring. Avoid it if you suffer from a bad back.

for him ★★☆

This position reduces the amount of force needed to thrust because it means you don't have to push too far. It allows for shallow thrusts that won't exhaust you and can last for as long as your woman has the strength to keep her back curved. Don't expect her to last too long in this position, though.

Female surrender
Many women instinctively open their legs wide for penetration and, with this gesture, offer themselves to a lover. The Yawning Posture and variations allow for such surrender.

THE YAWNING POSTURE

for him ☆☆

Your great advantage is that you are looking down, able to see powerful sexual emotion on your lover's face. Although your movement is impeded by the barrier of her thighs, it's worth remembering that not all erotic stimulation is about localized genital friction. Good sex includes the idea of sex as well as the actuality.

What begins as a straightforward man-on-top position can evolve quite easily into the Yawning Posture. By lifting her legs and opening her thighs, the woman enables her man to place his knees on either side of her hips and lean gently against her to thrust.

for her ☆☆

Although this position feels erotic, it does not provide you with too much sensation. The barrier of your uplifted thighs doesn't allow for deep penetration, so your clitoris will not receive much stimulation. However, the undeniable eroticism and helplessness you feel in this position can be a powerful turn-on.

THE CRAB'S POSITION

To get into this pleasurable position, the woman bends her knees and draws her thighs to her stomach (like a crab retracting its claws). When "letting go" playfully in positions like this, we get to know each other's innermost feelings and likes and dislikes.

for her ★★★★

By bending and drawing back your knees, you make the muscles in your upper thighs contract. Every push your partner makes on your knees transfers to the thighs and on to the genital area, so that each thrust heightens your pelvic tension and enjoyment.

for him ★★★

This particular position helps constrict the vagina around the penis and therefore offers a little more localized sensation than the Widely Opened Position. Help yourself to thrust more rhythmically by holding your partner's knees against your chest.

THE LOTUSLIKE POSITION

To get into the Lotuslike Position, the woman crosses her legs and draws them up toward her torso before the man leans over to penetrate her. This position may be a joke, since the strain imposed on the limbs makes it highly unlikely to be pleasurable. The few who can meet such a challenge may find it hard to sustain such a difficult position for very long.

for him ☆

The tangle of limbs desperately trying to stay in position beneath you is almost certain to put you off your stroke. There's a serious possibility of getting kicked in super-sensitive parts—assuming that you are able to get anywhere near your goal—so unless you are very brave, confine your enjoyment to looking at this picture.

for her

In theory, the result of adopting this familiar yoga position is to draw the vagina up to meet the penis. It may indeed be possible for a very supple, yoga-experienced individual to actually carry out the maneuver. But, you have to ask yourself, would it be worth it?!

VARIANT YAWNING

You are most likely to adopt this position after trying the original Yawning Posture *(p.30)*, since it feels much more comfortable. It's also a more satisfactory position for the man because it combines the ease of the missionary position with deeper penetration. With the calves of her legs resting on the man's shoulders, the woman can hold her legs high in the air, adding an element of powerful eroticism for both partners.

for him ★★★

This is a tiring position for you because your arms must support much of your weight as you thrust from a semi-upright position. It is unlikely that you will be able to sustain this position for very long. However, it does enable you to thrust farther inside your woman, which may make up for the fatigue.

for her ★★

Because of the extreme depth of penetration, you must be fully aroused and your vagina completely dilated before moving into this position. The local sensation of the thrust and withdrawal of the penis is very sexy, but there is no direct stimulation of the clitoris. Unless you react with extreme arousal to pressure put on the perineum and anal area, you are unlikely to climax this way.

Thrust techniques

According to the *Kama Sutra*, a man has a duty to satisfy his partner, and Vatsyayana included specific advice on how to use the penis as a kind of vibrator to give a woman immense arousal. Here are some of the sensual movements that the *Kama Sutra* recommends:

- **Blow of the Bull:** rubbing the penis along one side of the vagina
- **Blow of the Boar:** rubbing the penis along both sides of the vagina
- **Pressing:** pushing forcefully against the vagina
- **Sporting of the Sparrow:** moving the penis rapidly and lightly in and out of the vagina
- **Moving forward:** straightforward penetration
- **Piercing:** penetrating the vagina from above and pushing against the clitoris
- **Churning:** holding and moving the penis in the vagina
- **Giving a blow:** removing the penis and striking the vagina with it

Squeezing

By squeezing her vaginal muscles, the woman can intensify both her own pleasure and that of her man. Certain positions automatically constrict the muscles, and in others particular moves vary the pressure with which muscles caress the penis, producing exquisite, intensely exciting sensations.

How orgasm works

In the buildup of sexual excitement, tension is vital. Orgasm is the relief of this sexual tension. Without enough tension, orgasm is very difficult and sometimes impossible to achieve. The areas around the pelvis, in particular the thighs and buttocks, become a focus of sexual tension, and it is possible to aid and enhance climax by deliberately building this up. Bioenergetic exercises such as flexing the thighs and buttocks, or practicing Kegel exercises (p.36), all assist in achieving orgasm.

WIFE OF INDRA

This position, named after Indrani, the wife of the Hindu god Indra, is mentioned in the *Kama Sutra* as being suitable for the "highest congress"—lovemaking in which the vagina is fully open to allow for maximum penetration. The woman bends her knees and draws them up to her body. The man lifts her hips to penetrate her from a kneeling position, holding on to her thighs to control his thrusts.

for him ★★★★

This is a supremely comfortable kneeling sex position for you if your weight and height are compatible with your partner's. If your bodies align well, you can lean against her and thrust without straining your arms or legs.

for her ★★★

You can achieve considerable arousal by tensing your vaginal muscles, which happens when the knees are bent and drawn up in this way. A deep sexual tension builds up in the pelvic area that can explode into orgasm. This tension can be intensified if you are excited by being bundled up into a package, as perhaps Indra's wife, Indrani, felt.

The use of sorcery & magic

Vatsyayana wasn't averse to a little sorcery, and his original manuscript included spells and potions to give sexual advantage. Here are some of the least unpleasant. Although they are not recommended for 21st-century readers, it is fascinating to read about them.

HOW TO SLEEP WITH COUNTLESS WOMEN

Crush together shringataka (a substance never heard of by this author), jasmine, and wild figs and mix with licorice, sugar, and milk. Cook the mixture over a low heat with ghee (clarified butter) before dividing it into cakes. Eat the cakes and you will sleep with hordes of women—or so he promises! Since licorice and figs are known laxatives, you are, in reality, more likely to take up residence in the littlest room of the house.

HOW TO RUIN YOUR RIVAL'S CHANCES

This is a useful spell for any wife who has been supplanted in her husband's affections. The spell is intended to destroy the rival's "bhaga." The term bhaga has two meanings: "luck" and "vagina." To ruin a rival's bhaga is to render her barren and, therefore, in the context of the 4th century AD, absolutely useless as a wife.

The woman must obtain some of her rival's hair, a discarded toothpick, and a garland worn by the victim. These three items are wrapped in a piece of sacrificial cow's hide and buried under three large stones. Remnants of the garland are ground up, mixed with any remaining strands of hair, bound with black thread, and also buried. When they are all dug up, your rival's bhaga will shrink!

HOW TO HOLD ON TO YOUR MAN'S AFFECTIONS

The woman is advised to cast a spell to invoke the powers of Indrani (see opposite), considered to be the personification of marital bliss.

First, throw beans (symbolizing testicles) onto the head of your man. Then make an effigy of him and throw burning arrows (symbolizing the phallus) around it. This procedure is guaranteed to bring the man over to your side. A little extra magical advice is that if a couple desires a pale-skinned son, they must drink milk and eat rice cooked in milk. On this premise, if you desire instead a dark-skinned son, then you might feast on plain chocolate and black olives!

Today's magic is, alas, far more mundane. Viagra is one option, the contraceptive pill another, and the powers of counseling a third.

This 18th-century Indian miniature shows a lovers' elixir being prepared.

Practicing Kegel exercises

Kegel exercises are named after Dr. Arnold Kegel, who invented these techniques to help women restore the tone of the pubococcygeal (PC) muscles in the vagina after the birth of a baby. Toning the muscles in this area has the added advantage of intensifying sexual stimulation, since the more profoundly you are able to contract vaginally, the deeper your orgasm can be felt.

To locate your PC muscles, try to stop the flow of urine next time you go to the bathroom. Practice this several times to get used to controlling and toning these muscles. Now find out how strong your PC muscles are. Lie down on your back, place a finger inside your vagina, and contract the PC muscles again.

If the contractions are very faint, you must practice the following exercises regularly. Do these three simple routines anywhere, any time.

• The main Kegel exercise consists of slowly drawing the muscles in the vagina up for three seconds, relaxing for three seconds, then repeating. Repeat ten times on three separate occasions every day.

• Squeeze the muscles fast so that your vagina "flutters." Repeat ten times, three times a day.

• Imagine that inside your vagina is an elevator and your muscles must take it up four "floors." Draw the muscles up slowly, stopping briefly at each floor. Hold the muscles at the top for a little while, then release down to the ground floor again. Do this exercise twice a day.

HALF-PRESSED

This balletic position looks more like a movement in a gymnastics display than the wholehearted enjoyment of love. The woman stretches one leg out past her partner's body and bends the other leg at the knee, placing the sole of her foot on his chest. This action exposes her clitoris enough to give her the chance of clitoral stimulation, which she may not get in the Pressed Position. Stretching in itself is a sexy activity, which can add to the man's arousal.

for him ☆☆☆

Encourage your partner to move carefully against you so that the shaft of the penis receives some extra vaginal vibrations. You can also take the opportunity to caress her foot while you thrust. Foot touching feels both friendly and intimate and can in itself be sexually arousing.

for her ☆☆

To enhance the sensations you feel, roll your pelvis up against your man so that your clitoris is stimulated. As this position constricts the vagina, ask him not to thrust too hard, or you may feel discomfort rather than pleasure.

PRESSED

The woman must draw her legs up and place both feet on her partner's chest to achieve this submissive position. Like the Half-Pressed Position, the man must be careful not to thrust too hard into his lover's shortened vagina.

for him ✩✩✩

With your partner in a position of such complete surrender, you will feel very aroused by her vulnerability and your powerful strength. Caress her feet and gently hold on to one of her knees to help you thrust.

for her ✩✩

Lying in this defenseless position may bring erotic, subconscious feelings to the surface while you make love. As you watch your partner show his emotions, caress his thighs in rhythm with his thrusting movements.

THE SPLITTING OF A BAMBOO

This acrobatic position calls for the woman to fold and unfold her legs during intercourse, and so requires considerable suppleness. The sequence is repeated again and again: the woman raises one leg and puts it on her partner's shoulder; then, after a while, she brings that leg down and raises the other. Thus she "splits the bamboo." Such energetic movements remind me of the way young couples have fun inventing and reinventing crazy love positions during the first, intense moments of their relationships.

for him☆☆☆

As your woman raises each leg in turn, your penis is squeezed first by one set of vaginal muscles and then another, producing some very unusual sensations!

for her

This position makes your partner feel wonderful, so help him to focus on his pleasure while you have fun testing the limits of your suppleness.

FIXING A NAIL

By placing her heel on her man's forehead, the woman's leg and foot echo the shape of a hammer hitting a nail—the man's head! This is a fun position, and is meant to be enjoyed in a lighthearted manner.

for him ☆

As you thrust, her raised leg will move, varying the degree of sexual tension and sensation between vagina and penis. However, not every man is eager to have a foot resting against his forehead.

for her

Although this is not a deeply satisfying position for you, enjoy watching the emotions on your partner's face as he discovers some unusual sensations.

THE RISING POSITION

The woman needs to raise her feet up straight above the man's shoulders so that he can kneel in front of her and introduce his penis into her vagina. By keeping her thighs pressed together, the woman does most of the work, producing exquisite sensations for both partners.

for him ☆☆☆☆

Try this position if you feel seriously tired or even incapacitated, as well as for the pleasure of it. Since your partner's calves and feet are within easy reach of your hands, you can caress them or hold them to steady yourself while thrusting vigorously from beneath.

for her ☆☆☆☆

By using the pressure of your thighs to squeeze the penis, you can increase the friction between the vagina and penis and heighten the intensity of your—and his—sexual excitement.

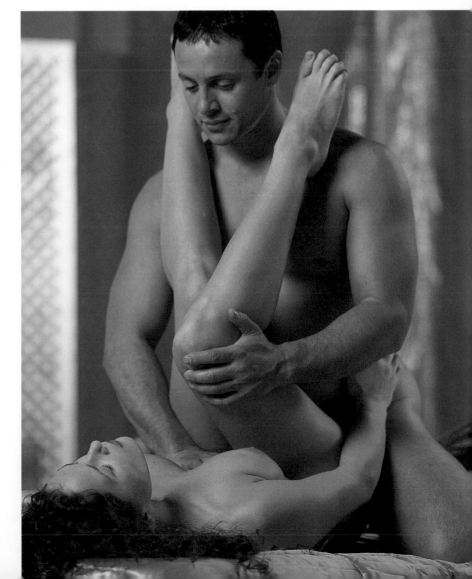

Full-body embraces *Drawing your lover close in these embraces enhances intimacy. Scientific tests show that human touch has life-affirming and life-enhancing properties, and thus it makes sense to believe that lovers relate better if they adore holding each other tight.*

CLASPING POSITION

Due to the frantic pace of our lives in the 21st century, modern lovers may need to learn the value of slow, languid lovemaking, of simply sliding in and out of a lover's embrace. With legs and arms intertwined, this position offers full body-to-body contact, encouraging an intense, passionate embrace.

for him ✰✰
The emphasis here is on closeness, and only a little movement should be necessary to enable you to sustain your erection.

for her ✰
Hold your man tight to gain the most physical and emotional pleasure from this passive position.

SIDE-BY-SIDE CLASPING

Such a loving embrace as this is reassuring and sensual, especially if there is any anxiety associated with sex. The act of simply wrapping yourself lovingly around your partner generates feelings of comfort and tenderness, and provides a gentle start to sex. The *Kama Sutra* suggests that the man lie on his left side and the woman on her right, but we aren't so prescriptive in the 21st century. Choose whichever side feels comfortable for you both.

for him and her☆☆

With your legs intertwined and your hands caressing each other's bodies, you will feel both protected and protective. Your senses will come alive as your skin is stroked, enabling you to relax and begin slow, unhurried love.

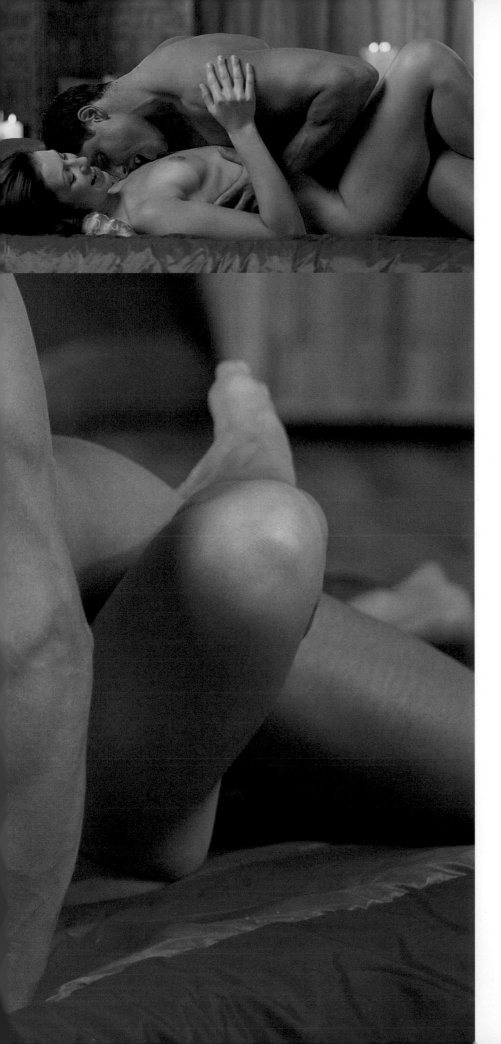

Entwining

Weaving and twining yourself around your partner forms part of the intricate, unspoken choreography of love, and enables you to get as close to each other as humanly possible. Such full-body touch and friction inevitably triggers feelings of powerful sexual excitement for both of you.

TWINING POSITION

A variation on the Pressing Position (p.44), the Twining Position requires the woman to place one leg across her lover's thigh in order to draw him as close to her as possible.

for him and her ☆☆

As both of you become aroused, your nipples harden, your muscles begin to tense, and the labia, clitoris, and penis all become erect. As your excitement increases, the breast tissue in both of you swells, sometimes creating a red flush across the chest area.

Pressing poses *Wonderful lovemaking in various embraces and positions can sometimes flow effortlessly, like a rhythmical dance. The Twining Position on pages 42–43 leads naturally into this position, with the thrilling result that every part of the body feels alive.*

THE PRESSING POSITION

for him☆☆☆☆

Value the body contact that Pressing offers, for in terms of arousal, you really come alive. As you react to your partner's intimate touch, your skin will tingle and the tension in the muscles mounts. The more you caress each other's skin and roll around, the greater the sexual charge.

for her☆☆

Let your man know how important his body contact is to you by moaning and crying out loud. Don't be afraid to arch your back if that is how the mood takes you. If your man rolls around, let your body follow.

Here, the woman grips her partner with her thighs so that her vagina and pelvic muscles tighten around his penis. There's nothing easier than sliding into intercourse in this position.

Vatsyayana's advice for effective courtship

Much of the original *Kama Sutra* contained advice on how to court a future wife in order to win her love and boost her confidence. Vatsyayana advised that a groom should be kind and generous toward his bride-to-be in order to win her trust.

GAMES

In the 4th century AD, a courtship began when the bride was still a young girl, so playing childish games was suggested as a way of establishing an early friendship with a girl bride-to-be. Today's psychologists would agree with this approach (only for grown-ups, of course). Playing games is a kind of rehearsal, a method of allowing you to make mistakes in a safe climate so that you learn new skills for the future. For the readers of this book, I've transposed some of Vatsyayana's ideas to more mature activities. You might go for storytelling—read to each other in bed, watch erotic movies, swap fantasies, or act out a fantasy.

GIFTS

Indian lovers in the 4th century AD were generous. Even a distant relative of the betrothed girl would receive a gift. The most popular gifts offered to the lady herself were flowers, betel nuts, trinkets, games, toys, and jewels. Each flower had its own meaning—blue hyacinths meant "I love you tenderly," daffodils expressed affection, jonquils signified returned affection, and orchids symbolized passion.

BEHAVIOR

Vatsyayana had different ideas than we do about how a woman should behave during courtship. She should not initiate any move or show willingness until her lover was ready to make a move. Nor should she offer any resistance when her intended

Seducing with gifts
This image from the Gita Govinda *depicts Krishna approaching his lover Radha with a gift of an exotic flower.*

husband made a pass. "Do not anticipate your man's desires," wrote Vatsyayana, "and let him show you love. Experience his loving as if it were something completely new for you. Appear reluctant even when he kisses you. Respond only when he embraces you by force."

Today's behavior gurus would recommend you don't overdo feigning reluctance since, if you continue to kiss a woman who shows no response, the activity becomes boring and off-putting.

THE RIGHT PARTNER

Vatsyayana believed it better to choose a mate compatible in social class and temperament. He believed this was more important than marrying someone because they are rich.

TURNING POSITION

"Congress having once commenced, passion alone gives birth to all the acts of the parties."

Kama Sutra

Many people can and do vary their movements spontaneously during sex; there's no law to say you should remain stuck in one position. The Turning Position will appeal to anyone who enjoys sexual exploration. Here the man makes a 180-degree turn without withdrawing his penis from the vagina.

for him and her ☆

According to Vatsyayana, this position takes a little practice to master. Even when perfected, it may not be the most erotic position, but you will certainly feel as if you have pushed the boundaries of sensuality.

180-DEGREE TURN

Throughout the sequence, the man supports himself on his arms to hold his torso clear of his partner. Begin in the missionary position, with the man's legs between the woman's. Without withdrawing his penis, the man lifts his right and then left leg over the woman's left leg. The woman can help by supporting his chest with her hands.

The man moves his legs around until his body is at a right angle to that of his partner. She parts her legs slightly to make it easier for him to remain inside her.

The man continues to move his torso toward the woman's head until he faces away from her with his legs on either side of her body.

ELEPHANT POSTURE

Vatsyayana suggests seeking inspiration from the mating habits of other members of the animal kingdom. By doing so, imaginative lovers can greatly extend their repertoire and gain an extra eroticism in their lovemaking. In this position, inspired by the mating techniques of elephants, the idea of the man entering the woman from the rear can be thrilling.

for him ★★★

You can rear up from your woman with the small of your back arched inward as you thrust deeply in this position. The animalistic power this affords you should add to your excitement.

for her ★★

This may be not the sexiest of lovemaking positions for you, since your clitoris receives little stimulation. However, the very idea of this pose can prove to be highly seductive. Press your thighs together to increase the sexual friction and sensations for you both.

The Chakras: centers of energy

Yogis believe that there are seven invisible centers of vital energy in the astral body, known as chakras. The astral body exists within and around the physical body. Five chakras are located at different points along the spine. The sixth is located at the middle of the forehead—the third eye—and the seventh is situated on the crown of the head.

Sexual activity is one way of arousing the awesome untapped energy known as *kundalini* that lies dormant at the base of the spine. *Kundalini* is often depicted as a coiled serpent. A person trained in yoga can awaken this force and direct it through each chakra to revitalize both body and spirit. The ability to control the flow of *kundalini* is regarded as a means of achieving *moksha*—a release from the cycle of life and death. *Moksha* can also mean ultimate sexual realization.

Female control *A woman in control doesn't have to be a dominatrix. Instead, her movements can be used to nurture her man, giving him the benefit of her powerfully feminine energy.*

MARE'S POSITION

Contrary to its name, the Mare's Position is not one of Vatsyayana's animal-inspired postures, but describes instead the maternal side of lovemaking, in which the female takes care of the male. It is more a technique than a position, in which the woman uses her vaginal muscles to squeeze the penis repeatedly, as if milking it. There are several positions in which this technique works well. The man-on-top Clasping Position *(p.40)* is best for some, but others find it more enjoyable to have the woman sitting astride the man, facing either away from or toward him.

for him ✩✩✩
Suggest the Mare's Position to your woman if you are feeling unwell, infirm, or if you just want a change. Perhaps she will offer you this penile treat anyway.

for her ✩✩
Use the second Kegel exercise on page 36 ("fluttering") to produce the rippling motion of your vaginal muscles. This will hopefully drive your man wild and give you many pleasurable sensations.

THE PAIR OF TONGS

With her knees bent, the woman faces her man as she sits astride him while he lies down. She draws his penis into her and repeatedly squeezes it with the muscles of her vagina, holding it tight for a long time. Penetration in this position is deep.

for her ✩✩✩✩

By sitting astride your man, you can stimulate yourself as well as him. If he doesn't wish to be totally passive, he can use his hands to stroke and caress you or use his fingers to stimulate your clitoris. If you like, you can stimulate your clitoris yourself, but you may prefer to focus entirely on vaginal movements. A few women can climax solely by doing this.

for him ✩✩

You will be greatly aroused by your partner making love to you, and will enjoy the sensations generated by your penis being squeezed inside her vagina.

Touching her intimately

Vatsyayana suggests that for the first three nights of marriage a couple should merely sleep together without the woman touching the man. Then he can make small moves to foster intimacy:
• As you talk and caress, move on to kissing (*see also pp.18–19*).
• Then slowly, delicately, slide your hands onto the tip of her breasts but go no farther. Wait.
• If she does not object and appears to like the touch, go on slowly, moving your hands farther.
• Gradually let your hands drift downward. If she objects, suggest that you turn this into a game. Touch your woman and ask her how the touch feels and where she would like you to move your hands next.

THE TOP

This is seriously dangerous and is presumably included in the *Kama Sutra* as a joke. My advice is to steer clear of it. According to Vatsyayana, the movement requires some dexterity (that's putting it mildly) and is achieved only with practice. While sitting astride her partner, the woman raises her legs clear of his body and swivels around on his penis. As she performs this maneuver she should take care not to lose her balance, otherwise she may hurt herself and her partner.

for him and her

Although just about feasible in theory, this position is difficult and hazardous in reality. Perhaps Indian women in Vatsyayana's time were much lighter and more muscular than females today, but they would also have needed to be skillful acrobats to carry out this move without damaging their man.

THE SWING

for him ★★★

The swinging movements of your woman across the head of your penis are especially sensual for you. She will need to learn to judge how far forward she can swing before your penis slips out of her vagina.

for her ☆

This position makes your partner feel wonderful, but has less to offer you by way of stimulation. You may be aroused by the repeated friction of the penis moving in and out of your vagina.

This is an uncomplicated woman-on-top position. The woman sits with her back to the man and swings forward and backward by bending her elbows up and down, consecutively covering and uncovering his penis as she moves. The original *Kama Sutra* suggests that the man lie with his back arched, but since this would only be practical if he possesses superhuman strength, it is wiser for him to lie flat or lean back on his hands.

Standing

Lovemaking while standing seemed to hold a special meaning in ancient Indian culture. Standing couples appear frequently in the erotic sculptures adorning ancient temples, and there is a certain grace evident in these entwined vertical poses.

THE SUSPENDED CONGRESS

The man leans against a wall and lifts the woman up by locking his hands underneath her buttocks or holding her thighs. The woman needs to grip her man with her legs, as if riding a horse, and may need to facilitate his moves of thrusting forward and backward.

for her ☆☆

If it is hard for your man to keep a sensual rhythm going, increase your pleasure by pushing off from the wall with your feet to give the position more support and to maintain the rhythm of lovemaking.

for him ☆

This position is not one for the over-voluptuous in figure, since you require a lot of strength to pull your woman to you and then relax in sequential moves.

"In all these things connected with love, everybody should act according to his own inclination."

Kama Sutra

THE SUPPORTED CONGRESS

When passion suddenly overwhelms us, we may desire spontaneous sex standing in the nearest available private space. Lovers can achieve this position by leaning against a wall or into one another. If the woman is shorter than the man, he can bend his knees or she can stand on his feet or on tiptoe. This is not guaranteed to work if there is a major height difference.

for him ★★★★
This can be an outrageously exciting position for you. Because you are supported by the wall or braced against your woman, you can thrust freely and passionately.

for her ★★★
Lift your thigh up against your man's to achieve greater penetration as he thrusts, which will enhance your enjoyment of this position.

CONGRESS OF A COW

In this challenging position, the woman bends over and places one or both hands on the ground for support. The man then "mounts" her from behind to penetrate her. He needs to hold her hard against him so that he can pull her backward and forward.

for him ★★★
This move allows for deep penetration and enables you to control the depth and power of your thrusts for maximum pleasure.

for her ★★
As your man thrusts, he can move his fingers around to your clitoris and stroke it in rhythm with his thrusting. Focus on the sensation of his hips pounding against your buttocks and his penis sliding across your sensitive perineum, and don't be afraid to use your own fingers if you want to.

Ananga Ranga

Sitting positions

In the Ananga Ranga *the term for sex in sitting positions is* upavishta. *Depending on your frame of mind,* upavishta *can be youthful, charged with eroticism, comic, or even acrobatic.*

THE LOTUS POSITION

The Lotus Position is described as a favorite in the *Ananga Ranga* and, despite its tricky-sounding yogalike name, it isn't too difficult to do. It calls for quite a lot of male strength, since the man will need to use his arms to help his woman move up and down on his penis. She sits on his knee, carefully lowering herself onto his penis, then extends her legs out behind him. Experiment with the most comfortable position for her legs; if she prefers to initiate the action herself instead of being subject to her man moving her body, she will probably find that a kneeling position works better.

for him ★★★★

If lifting your woman up and down becomes tiring, ask her to kneel with her feet on either side of your thighs so that she can push off without your involvement. This allows you to relax and enjoy yourself completely.

for her ★★

If your man grasps you sensitively around the buttocks, he can help lift you every time you move up and down. Do encourage him to caress you to increase your passion.

THE ACCOMPLISHING POSITION

The Accomplishing Position is a natural development of the Lotus Position. Leaning on one hand for support and balance, the woman keeps one leg lifted while making love. This creates a different angle between the penis and vagina and alters the tension felt by both lovers.

for her ★★

This face-to-face position can be tender and loving, as you can kiss your man and show him affection.

for him ★★

This is a warm, friendly embrace with pleasing sensations, but you have limited thrusting movements.

This position also involves the man lifting his woman and moving her around on his penis, and thus works best when performed by a strong man and light woman. With the woman's legs hanging over the man's elbows, he moves her from side to side—or forward and back in a variation known as the Monkey Position.

THE CRYING OUT POSITION

for her☆☆☆☆

This is a surprisingly arousing stroke for you because it puts pressure on a number of sensitive spots on the outer entrance of the vagina.

for him☆☆

Although this is not a deeply satisfying position for you, it makes your partner feel wonderful and very aroused.

The four orders of women

The author of the *Ananga Ranga*, Kalyana Malla, classified women according to their temperament and identified four different types, all of whom sound very different from their 21st-century counterparts.

THE PADMINI

"She, in whom the following signs and symptoms appear, is called Padmini, or Lotus-woman. Her face is pleasing as the full moon; her body, well clothed with flesh, is soft as the Shiras (a tall, fragrant tree) or mustard flower; her skin is fine, tender and fair as the yellow lotus, never dark-colored, though resembling, in the effervescence and purple light of her youth, the cloud about to burst. Her Yoni (vulva) resembles the opening lotus-bud, and her Kama-salila (vaginal secretion, thought to be "the water of life," the counterpart of semen) is perfumed like the lily, which has newly burst. She walks with a swan-like gait, and her voice is low and musical as the note of the Kokila bird (the Indian cuckoo); she delights in white raiment, in fine jewels and in rich dresses."

THE SHANKINI

"The Shankini, or Conch-woman, is of bilious temperament, her skin being always hot and tawny, or dark yellow-brown; her body is large, her waist thick, and her breasts small. Her Yoni is ever moist with Kama-salila which is distinctly salt and the cleft is covered with thick hair."

THE CHITRINI

"The Chitrini, or Art-woman, is of middle size, neither short nor tall, with bee-black hair, thin, round, shell-like neck; tender body; waist lean-girthed as the lion's; hard, full breasts; well-turned thighs and heavily made hips. The hair is thin about the Yoni, the Mons Veneris being soft, raised and round. The Kama-salila is hot, and has the perfume of honey, producing from its abundance, a sound during the venereal rite. Her eyes roll, and her walk is coquettish, like the swing of an elephant."

THE HASTINI

"The Hastini, or Elephant-woman, is short of stature; she has a stout coarse body, and her skin, if fair, is of dead white; her hair is tawny, her lips are large; her voice is harsh, choked, and throaty and her neck is bent. Her gait is slow, and she walks in a slouching manner: often the toes of one foot are crooked. Her Kama-salila has the savor of the juice which flows in spring from the elephant's temples."

An alluring Indian lover, possibly a Padmini, painted in the 18th century.

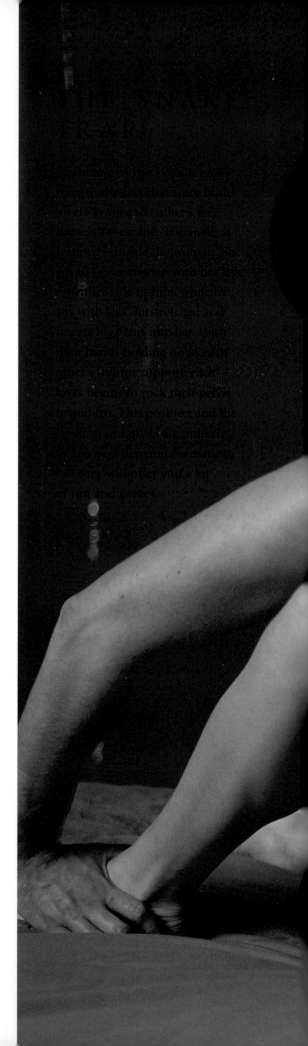

THE POSITION OF EQUALS

This is another woman-on-top position *(upavishta)* that needs a degree of fitness if you are to perform it enjoyably. According to the *Ananga Ranga*, it is the man who should position the woman's legs once she is seated astride his lap. However, as you move out of the straightforward sitting posture from which this position usually develops, either partner can make the adjustment to ensure that their passion is sustained. The woman can grasp her man's waist with her legs by locking them together behind his back.

for him ✩✩
As your woman leans back, she can use her buttock and thigh muscles to set up a pleasurable jazz rhythm on your penis.

for her ✩
The *Ananga Ranga* suggests that your man clasps his hands around your neck, but he can use his hands to much better effect by stroking and caressing your breasts. Ask him to kiss your breasts instead if it gives you more pleasure.

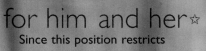

for him and her ☆

Since this position restricts thrusting, it's probably best enjoyed as a physical respite when you are tired, or as love play when you feel like "messing around."

"There are three forces of carnal desire (Vega). These are: furious appetite, a moderate desire and slow kindling"

Ananga Ranga

THE PAIRED FEET POSITION

The woman lowers herself down onto the man's penis as he sits with his legs wide apart. Once they are in position and he has penetrated her fully, he presses her thighs together with his hands while he thrusts into her.

for him ☆☆☆

You can increase the pleasurable sensations of your penis being squeezed by your woman's constricted vagina if you keep her thighs pressed together.

for her ☆

As you lean back on your elbows, you gain the perfect opportunity to gaze into your lover's face and watch his excitement. Face-to-face positions like this can be emotionally arousing for you even though you may not be greatly stimulated physically.

Kneeling & lying

In the Ananga Ranga, positions in which the woman lies on her back as the man kneels to enter her are known as uttana-bandha. She feels an erotic sense of helplessness as he moves her into the most comfortable position to suit his powerful need to penetrate her deeply.

THE LEVEL FEET POSTURE

The woman lies on her back and the man raises her body so her buttocks rest on his thighs. He braces himself against her and positions her legs on his shoulders, grasps her waist, and pulls her up onto his penis.

for him ★★★★

Because your woman's buttocks are raised, you can penetrate her deeply, which will be highly pleasurable for you. A word of warning: make sure you do not inadvertently hurt her.

for her ★★★

To increase your own pleasure, close your thighs tightly so that your vagina constricts and you experience his thrusting as intensely as possible.

The G-spot

The G-spot is a highly sensitive area at the far end of the vagina on the front wall. The area is named after a gynecologist, Dr. Ernst Grafenburg, who was the first man to locate and write about it. When it is pressed firmly and consistently, the G-spot can trigger orgasm and, in a few women, a kind of ejaculation of thin fluid. An analysis of this ejaculate by an Israeli research team showed that the fluid was very similar to seminal fluid except, of course, that it did not contain sperm. Not every woman appears to possess a G-spot, and its existence is hotly contested. It is difficult to locate your own G-spot unless you use a slim vibrator; G-spot vibrators pulsate rather than vibrate on the grounds that pulsation works much better on this area!

THE RAISED FEET POSTURE

The *Ananga Ranga* describes this posture thus: lying on her back, the woman bends her legs at the knees and draws them back "as far as her hair." Her partner then enters her from a kneeling position.

for her ☆☆☆☆

You can gain considerable pleasure by raising your hips so that your partner penetrates you at an angle in which his penis stimulates your highly sensitive G-spot. You may also like to encourage him to use his hands to caress you and fondle your breasts.

for him ☆☆

You will be able to penetrate deeply and become quickly aroused in this position. Since you are kneeling and do not need to use your hands to support yourself, use them to caress your partner lovingly.

THE REFINED POSTURE

This position allows for the deepest penetration so far. The woman lies with her legs bent on either side of her man's hips. He raises her up by lifting her buttocks with his hands so that he can position her at the best angle in which to thrust into her very effectively.

for her★★★★

If you like the idea, ask your lover to gently lift your buttocks up and away from the anus and perineum to offer you erotic sensations. You may also prefer him to use his free hand to caress your face and body, which is powerfully exciting for you.

for him★★★★

Although you are highly aroused by deep penetration, other parts of your body can benefit from sexual stimulation, too. Encourage your lover to reach up to gently fondle your nipples, chest, and shoulders as you make love in this position.

THIS HITS THE SPOT

KAMA'S WHEEL

The woman sits astride her lover with her legs extended. The man sits with his legs outstretched and grasps his lover securely behind her shoulder blades. Their outstretched limbs create a spokelike pattern that gives the position its name. Ideally, the woman should be able to lean back and move just enough to keep the man's penis erect, thus allowing both lovers to focus only on this erotic moment and blot out all other concerns.

for him and her☆☆

The concept of Kama's Wheel is different from our 21st-century attitudes to sex and needs a little explanation. This is not a position that provides fierce erotic stimulation leading to rapid orgasm. Instead, it's intended to be used as a type of sexual meditation to bring a high level of awareness, a sharpness of appetite, and an increased sense of well-being. The ultimate aim of this sexual state is to bring about a balance of mind that is clear, calm, and happy.

Tantric ecstasy

Tantric philosophy postdates all the scripts from which the original *Kama Sutra* and *Ananga Ranga* were taken, yet both books are imbued with Tantric concepts. Tantra draws on the belief that the more accomplished your sexual performance becomes, the better you become as a person. Put succinctly, the idea is that you can achieve an ecstatic sense of being through marvelous sex. When sex starts to reach an almost timeless stage—when each movement and every caress feels otherworldly—you are nearing "heaven," and the feeling you experience at that moment is like a powerful meditation. My own view is that although I believe that it *is* possible to achieve this state of bliss through passionate sex, I'm not convinced that you can do it by following prescribed sex routines. But I do believe we can have a lot of fun trying!

INTACT POSTURE

Fortunately, good sex generally means that anything goes; in other words, "Whatever you want to do (within reason) is OK by me if I love you." The Intact Posture is a position in which the woman is physically confined and the man is in control. She lies on her back with her legs bent in close to her body and her knees resting on her partner's chest. His knees are positioned outside her thighs and he needs to put one hand under her buttocks to lift her slightly before entering her.

for him ☆☆☆

This is a relatively easy position from which to thrust and enjoy making love with your partner.

for her ☆

If lack of control and helplessness are part of what turns you on, this could be extremely arousing mentally, although physically it is not massively satisfactory. After penetration, your man can support you on his thighs so that his hands are free to roam and explore your body.

THE PLACID EMBRACE

As the woman lies on her back, her legs on either side of her man, he kneels before her and lifts her hips up to meet his penis. She can draw her man closer to her by crossing her ankles behind his back, emphasizing her feelings of tenderness and intimacy.

for him and her ☆☆

As the man hugs the woman close to him, he can slip a pillow under her back so that she can thrust against him without hurting herself, increasing the levels of pleasure for them both.

How sexual response works: the 21st-century view

There are three main stages of sexual response: desire, when you begin to want your partner; arousal, when your sexual excitement mounts; and orgasm, which speaks for itself. It's possible to experience each of these stages on their own without experiencing any of the others, strange though that may seem.

Desire can happen as a result of a look, a touch, a suggestion. Arousal happens through sexual touch, foreplay, and lovemaking in general. Orgasm happens at the peak of excitement as a happy reflex of whole-body sensuality, although many people can also experience orgasm just by stimulating the genitals. After orgasm, the body generally returns slowly to its previous unstimulated state, except in the case of some women who find they are able to experience further orgasms a little later on.

...APING POSTURE

In this position, pillows or cushions are used to arch the [woman's] [body] and raise her up to the required height to meet her man. The clitoris is stretched and exposed at this [height] and angle, and is therefore more likely to be affected by the thrust and pull of intercourse. The man kneels between his lover's legs and, with his hands underneath her buttocks, pulls her forward onto his erect penis.

"If a man attempt any deed, he should do it with the spirit of a lion."

Ananga Ranga

for him ★★★

This is another dominant position in which you can thrust effectively while keeping your hands free to heighten your partner's pleasure.

for her ★★☆

Although pillows will position you well for clitoral stimulation as your man thrusts, the use of either his or your fingers during intercourse will make for much more effective stimulation. Don't be afraid to ask for this.

THE ENCIRCLING POSITION

The woman lies with her calves crossed while the man leans over to enter her. There are associations with bondage in this pose, which, combined with the fact that her pelvis is opened wide and her clitoris exposed, creates a risqué feeling that is very exciting.

for him☆☆☆☆

Your partner's openness will arouse your subconscious desires while you make love in this position, despite your not being able to penetrate too deeply.

for her☆☆

Your crossed legs put pressure on your thighs and raise the level of pelvic tension, which assists the buildup of excitement. Although the barrier of your legs prevents direct clitoral contact, if your man is able to move up close inside you, you may feel deep, internally sensual pressure on the G-spot.

"The slower desires of a woman mean she is not easily satisfied by a single act of congress." Ananga Ranga

THE SPLITTING POSITION

As the woman lies with her legs in the air, her partner enters her from a kneeling position. He then lifts her legs higher to rest them against his shoulder and begins to thrust. Meanwhile, she presses her knees and thighs together to constrict his penis.

for him ☆☆☆

Positions such as this, in which penetration is deep and the vagina is squeezed, are excellent for the older man who needs a robust sensation during intercourse. Your penis feels tight inside the vagina, while the gripping sensation of your lover's thighs gives you additional friction that may be necessary to bring you to orgasm.

for her ☆☆

Maximize your pleasure by keeping your knees and thighs pressed close together to constrict your vagina. This also increases the friction on your lover's penis.

The effects of aging on men

Clinicians now believe that as many as two-thirds of cases of male sexual dysfunction are caused by physical problems, many of which are a result of the aging process. Such problems include impotence, which may be caused by damage to the arteries that supply blood to the penis, and loss of erection, thought to be the result of weakening of the valves that hold the blood supply in the erect penis.

Hormonal changes, which are another aspect of the aging process, may also result in a lower sex drive and less genital sensation. When a lack of sensation causes problems during lovemaking, sex positions that offer much harder, stronger stimulation can prove to be very effective. For other, more serious conditions, medications such as Viagra can be of use, as may vacuum devices and penile rings, which can help to preserve an erection.

Side by side

The author of the Ananga Ranga included side-by-side poses called tiryak-bandha, *or transverse positions. These moves are for those times when either partner is tired, but still passionate, or when a woman is pregnant and does not want to put a lot of weight on her abdomen.*

CRAB EMBRACE

In the Crab Embrace, the man lies on his left side, places his right thigh across his woman's right thigh, and pulls her toward him. She places her left leg up over his buttocks and snuggles in close.

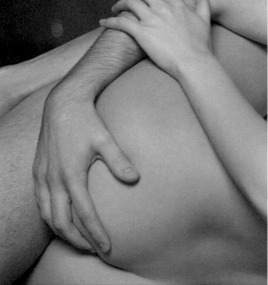

for her ☆

Since your man's right arm will be freed up, he can slide his hand up and down your back and buttocks with sensitive caresses as you make slow, unhurried love.

for him ☆

Your lover's right arm will be curved underneath your neck and around your shoulders in a gesture of intimacy, leaving her left arm free to roam your body.

THE TRANSVERSE LUTE

To achieve this position, the woman raises her leg slightly to allow her partner to enter her, and then he raises his leg and rests it on her thigh. Side-by-side positions are good for those men who need more friction during intercourse. The penis thrusts are felt along the insides of the labia, which are pressed against the penis by the woman's outstretched legs. These positions also give her an increased likelihood of arousal and orgasm.

for him ☆☆☆☆

If you need especially strong friction on your penis, you may achieve greater sensation by pulling yourself up slightly toward your woman's head so that the tip of your penis almost, but not quite, leaves the vagina every time you pull. This can be extremely exciting for both of you. It may also enable your penis to brush against her clitoris.

for her ☆☆☆☆

Penetration will naturally pull on one side of your vaginal opening and, if you are lying on your left side, this can be especially stimulating. Sex researchers Steve and Vera Bodansky believe that the left side of the clitoris is more sensitive than the right, and if this is accurate, it might also be that the left side of the vaginal opening is more sensitive, too.

Sexual tension and multiple orgasms

The various sitting positions suggested by the *Ananga Ranga* are useful for maintaining a degree of sexual tension over a long period of time. US therapists Hartman and Fithian suggest that it is this kind of slow, tantalizing approach that enables you to achieve a higher degree of sensual arousal. This, in turn, increases the likelihood of experiencing multiple orgasms. Men and women need a greater buildup of sexual tension if they are to enjoy multiple orgasms than they would do for a single climax.

The three orders of men

Like women, men are classified into various types according to their temperament in the *Ananga Ranga*: the Shasha, or Hare-man; the Vrishabha, or Bull-man; and the Ashwa, or Horse-man.

THE SHASHA

"The Shasha is known by a Linga (penis) which in erection does not exceed six finger-breadths (about 3 in/7.5 cm). His figure is short and spare but well proportioned in shape and make; he has small hands, knees, feet, loins and thighs, the latter being darker than the rest of the skin. His features are clear and well proportioned; his face is round, his teeth are short and fine, his hair is silky and his eyes are large and well opened. He is humble in his demeanor; his appetite for food is small, and he is moderate in his carnal desires. Finally, there is nothing offensive in his Kama-salila, or semen."

THE VRISHABHA

"The Vrishabha is known by a Linga of nine fingers in length (4½ in/11.5 cm). His body is robust and tough, like that of a tortoise; his chest is fleshy, his belly is hard, and the frogs of the upper arms are turned so as to be brought in front. His disposition is cruel and violent, restless and irascible, and his Kama-salila is ever ready."

A Shasha man makes love to a Padmini woman *(p.61)*.

This India School stone relief depicts the archetypal Vrishabha.

THE ASHWA

"The Ashwa is known by a Linga of twelve fingers (6 in/15 cm) long. He is tall and large-framed, but not fleshy, and his delight is in big and robust women, never in those of delicate form. He is reckless in spirit, passionate and covetous, gluttonous, volatile, lazy, and full of sleep. He cares little for the venereal rite, except when the spasm approaches. His Kama-salila is copious, salt and goat-like."

Woman on top

The author of the Ananga Ranga *advises that woman-on-top positions, or purvshayita-bandha (role-reversal positions), should be used if a man is tired or has not satisfied a woman. He was clearly aware of how women's sexual responses differ from those of men.*

THE ASCENDING POSITION

Kalyana Malla suggests in the *Ananga Ranga* that if a woman's "passion has not been gratified by previous copulation," she can sit cross-legged on her man's thighs, "seize" his penis, and insert it into her vagina, and then move herself up and down.

for her ★★★★

You can alter the angle of your partner's entry into your vagina to give yourself the stimulation you need to become highly aroused. This could be clitoral stimulation either from his penis or from your own fingers as you rise and fall above him. There's the added bonus of being able to control, to some extent, the contact between his penis and your G-spot.

for him ★★★

This method of intercourse is useful for men who suffer from initial erectile problems during intercourse. It is possible to tease a soft penis into the vagina, providing an appreciated starting point for you.

THE INVERTED EMBRACE

for her ✩✩✩

Being in control of the lovemaking will increase your excitement and allow you to absorb yourself in the sensations that give you both pleasure.

for him ✩✩

Your lover's swiveling hips produce a kind of churning, side-by-side movement, like a vigorous body massage, that feels wonderful and different from the usual thrust of intercourse.

The man lies back with his woman on top of him. She then inserts his penis into her vagina, presses her breasts to his, and moves her hips. She can steady herself by holding on to him.

THE ORGASMIC ROLE-REVERSAL

The woman squats on her man's thighs, inserts his penis, closes her legs firmly, and adopts a churning motion to "thoroughly satisfy herself."

for her ✩✩✩✩

The freedom of movement that this position brings will give you control over the speed, angle, and amount by which you move your pelvis around. Add variety to your erotic sensations by varying the depth of penetration.

for him ✩✩✩

This can be another useful method of initiating intercourse when your spirit is willing but your body is tired or reluctant.

The Perfumed Garden

The long...... The Perfumed Garden *describes 11 main poses that show the attention its author paid to physical differences between men and women. In this classic first position and its variations, a man with a long penis can easily adjust the depth of his thrusts so as not to hurt his partner if he "completely fills all her parts."*

FIRST POSTURE

The woman lies on her back and raises her knees, resting her legs across her man's thighs. He supports his weight on his hands and knees to ensure that he can control his thrusting carefully once he has entered her.

for her ☆☆

In this position it is possible for you to help yourself have an orgasm with self-stimulation if you find that intercourse alone doesn't bring you to climax.

"A man whose member gets strong and hard is relished and appreciated by women."

The Perfumed Garden

for him ✩✩✩

Use your toes to push against the bed as you thrust so you can control the power and rhythm of your lovemaking and maximize your pleasure.

GRIPPING WITH TOES

This position is probably best used as a transition from one move to another. The woman lies on her back and the man kneels between her thighs, places his hands on either side of her neck, and braces himself with his toes in order to keep his balance. She may wrap her legs around his waist and pull herself up on to his penis so that he can fully penetrate her.

for him and her ✩✩

Although the man is unable to thrust freely in this posture, he can vary the angle of penetration simply by leaning toward or away from his woman. This position can be used in an interlude between more vigorous lovemaking. Its gentler pace allows you both to focus on the intensity of the sensations you feel.

THE ONE WHO STAYS AT HOME

This loving technique is tiring, so is best used sparingly. In it a woman can demonstrate how hot she is for her man. She lies on her back with her knees bent and her feet and shoulders supporting her weight. The man leans over her and supports himself on his hands and knees. She pushes up on to the balls of her feet and lifts her hips to allow him to enter her, then drops her pelvis down suddenly. She continues to lift and drop her pelvis in quick succession, placing her hands on the floor on either side of her hips to steady herself if necessary (*see inset, right*).

for him ☆☆☆

As your partner makes love to you in this tantalizing way, follow her movements by sticking "like glue to her," taking care that your penis does not slip out completely. You may be quickly turned on by her controlling thrusts as she lies beneath you.

for her ☆☆☆

The very act of pushing your pelvis up to meet your lover as he comes down on you feels sexy and erotically empowering.

Inspiring affection in a woman

The Perfumed Garden gives its male readers a chance to consider carefully the words of a woman on the ideal way to inspire affection in the fairer sex:

"O you who question me, those things which develop the taste for coition are the toyings and touches which precede it, and then the close embrace at the moment of ejaculation! Believe me, the kisses, nibblings and suction of the lips, the close embrace, the visits of the mouth to the nipples of the bosom, and the sipping of the fresh saliva, these are the things to render affection lasting. In acting thus, the two orgasms take place simultaneously, and enjoyment comes to the man and woman at the same moment."

.....and the short!

These may not be the easiest or most natural of poses for a woman, but the author of The Perfumed Garden, *Sheikh Nefzawi, recommends them for a man whose "member is a short one."*

for him ★★☆

If you have a short penis, you will find that you gain satisfaction from penetrating your partner's constricted vagina. However, you should investigate alternatives to bring you to orgasm that provide both you and her with pleasure, such as mutual masturbation or oral sex, plus the use of sex aids.

for her

This is a supremely uncomfortable position to sustain. Tell your partner when you have had enough and move on to a more mutually satisfying position.

SECOND POSTURE

The woman lies on her back and raises her legs in the air. She draws her legs back and holds them apart with her hands, allowing her man to lean over her and move in close to her genitals. He kneels by her hips and places his hands on either side of her head for support before entering her.

Naming the female parts

Sheikh Nefzawi lavishes praise on the female sexual organs, and goes on to describe at length his fascination with the genitals of young women: "Such a vulva is very plump and round in every direction, with long lips, grand slit, the edges well divided and symmetrically founded; it is soft, seductive, perfect throughout. It is most pleasant and no doubt the best of all the different sorts. May God grant us the possession of such a vulva! Amen. It is warm, tight and dry; so much so that one might expect to see fire burst from it. Its form is graceful, its odor pleasant; the whiteness of its outside sets off its carmine-red middle. There is no imperfection about it."

THE STOPPERAGE

Slipping a pillow under her buttocks will help the woman support her back as she lies in this constricted position. The man kneels between her hips and leans forward against her bent legs, pressing her knees toward her breasts. This action pushes the cervix (the opening to the womb at the far end of the vaginal canal) forward, which can make penetration quite difficult. Once the man has inserted his penis, it is pressed against the cervix, as if stopping up a bottle with a cork. It is wise to heed Nefzawi's warning: to avoid hurting the woman, this position should be tried only by men with a short or soft penis.

for him ★★★
The outcome of this position is that the walls of your lover's vagina are pressed together, bringing you an intensity of sensation and pleasure.

for her ★★
You, too, feel a corresponding intensity of sensation—so much so that Nefzawi warns that this position may be painful for you. If you do feel any pain, it's important that you speak out and stop.

Deep penetration *Some couples enjoy, even need, very deep penetration from sexual intercourse, perhaps because the cervix or G-spot benefits from internal pressure. The Third Posture allows for full penetration, but ensure that the woman is prepared for it first.*

THIRD POSTURE

The man kneels between his lover's legs, then lifts her left leg up over his right shoulder and tucks her right leg under his left arm. He penetrates her in this position.

for him ☆☆☆☆

This position offers you such deep penetration and pleasure that it brings you heightened sensitivity and prolongs your erection.

for her ☆☆☆☆

Even the thought of this highly erotic position can prove to be very titillating to many women, but I recommend that you attempt it only when you are fully aroused. During sexual arousal the vagina undergoes a process called "tenting," in which the upper end enlarges so it can accommodate a deep-thrusting penis comfortably. You feel stretched wide open and may gain considerable pleasure from the experience.

THIS HITS THE SPOT

FITTING ON OF THE SOCK

This is a terrific position for the woman. Her man uses his penis as a dildo to arouse her in preparation for deep penetration. Try it before the Third Posture or other deep-thrusting positions. While she lies on her back with legs apart, he rests her buttocks on his thighs and inserts the tip of his penis into her vulva, which he then pulls closed gently with his thumb and first finger. He moves his penis back and forth sensitively to moisten the outer lips with his secretion before he penetrates her.

The unique woman

Here are some of the names given to women's genitals in *The Perfumed Garden*. You can sometimes discern their supposed qualities from the names alone—the voluptuous, the crusher, the glutton, the beautiful, the hot one, and the delicious one.

In describing women's genitalia in great detail, Sheikh Nefzawi displays not only a sense of humor, but also a recognition of something that many of us seem to have lost sight of today. Just as all faces are different, so too are genitalia—and personalities. The Sheikh uses these physical differences as a metaphor for the glorious variety within the nature of the female spirit.

for her ★★★★

Fitting on of the Sock can be extremely arousing, although a 21st-century variation is even better: you might persuade your man to use his penis not just around the vaginal opening, but also in a gentle rhythm around your clitoris. Many women can climax through this action alone.

for him ★★

This position is a tantalizing precursor to deep penetration, but is also a good method of lovemaking when you don't have much energy but want to satisfy your woman with incredible stimulation.

THIS HITS THE SPOT

Angles of entry
By varying the angle of penetration slightly, these positions, which can be performed as a sequence, provide each partner with the potential to enjoy a variety of deeply pleasurable sensations.

FOURTH POSTURE

The man kneels, positions his lover's legs over each of his shoulders, and raises her hips slightly. This allows him to explore the most pleasurable angles of penetration. The woman's sexual response can increase as he puts pressure on the different spots on her vagina.

WITH LEGS IN THE AIR

From the Fourth Posture, the man passes one of his lover's legs across his face so it rests beside the other, across his chest, as he penetrates her. He can also squeeze her buttocks together with his thighs so she is pressed hard onto his penis.

for him ✮✮✮

If you are an older man who requires vigorous pressure on the penis to achieve or maintain arousal, this position will provide enough stimulation to bring you to climax. Alternate forceful thrusts with gentle ones for maximum pleasure.

for her ✮

Squeeze your thighs together to increase your partner's pleasure. This posture doesn't provide much clitoral stimulation for you, so try it after a particularly stimulating position or oral sex to keep you satisfied.

TAIL OF THE OSTRICH

Intercourse is not as pleasurable in this position as in others, but the highly erotic experience of being in, or seeing your woman in, this unusual posture may fulfill some of your sexual fantasies. The man kneels by his woman's raised hips and lifts her legs, holding them against his chest as he enters her.

for him ✮✮✮

You can vary the sensations you feel by raising or lowering your lover's hips, which alters the depth and angle of penetration. As you do this, support the small of her back with your hand.

for her ✮✮

The most benefit to be gained from the Tail of the Ostrich is the rush of blood to the head that comes from being upside-down. This rush can intensify excitement and orgasm. Lying in this position can place undue pressure on your spine and neck, but if you are happy to indulge your man, then that's fine.

Lying together *In these simple side-by-side positions, you lie with your faces close together. This creates an intimate mood that inspires feelings of tenderness. Often these positions place no pressure on the woman's abdominal area, so are ideal for couples who are expecting a baby.*

FIFTH POSTURE

Both lovers lie with their legs outstretched. The woman rests her uppermost leg on top of her man's leg, bending it a little to allow him to enter her deeply. He pulls her toward him by grasping her hip and rolling her onto her side. By pulling her and then letting go a little, he rocks her on and off his penis.

for him and her ☆☆

The gentle, intimate way you make love in this position will enable you both to show your pleasure and desire for each other.

LOVE'S FUSION

Many lovers feel aroused by the sheer sensation of entwining their legs. Here, the woman hooks her leg directly over her lover's hip so her vagina is wide open for penetration. The Sheikh concludes his instructions to the man for this position with the words, "After having introduced your member you move as you please, and she responds to your action as she pleases."

for him ☆☆☆

Face-to-face positions such as this permit you to thrust vigorously to gain deep stimulation and satisfaction.

for her ☆☆☆

If you are not feeling strong, this is an easy and relaxed method of enjoying energetic intercourse. You can move in rhythm with your partner's thrusting to increase your arousal if you wish.

Naming the male parts

Sheikh Nefzawi makes an interesting character analysis of the male genitalia. Below are three of his most imaginative descriptions:

The Smith's Bellows "The member is so called on account of its alternate swelling and subsiding again. If swollen up, it stands erect and if not, it sinks down flaccid."

The Sleeper "When it gets into erection, it lengthens out and stiffens itself to such an extent that one might think it would never go soft again. But when it has left the vulva, after having satisfied its passion, it goes to sleep."

The Impudent "lifts impudently the clothing of its master by raising its head fiercely and makes him ashamed while itself feels no shame. It acts in the same unabashed way with women, turning up their clothes and laying bare their thighs."

RAINBOW ARCH

This is one of those mad positions that couples fall into when fooling around in extra-playful mode. It has more novelty value than pleasurable profit, but you never know—it might turn out to be the most erotic experience of your life. Before penetration, the man lies at right angles to his lover, puts his legs between hers, then moves his legs around so that she can reach his feet.

for her ☆☆
The unusual angle of entry provides novel sensations for you. You are literally touched from angles never otherwise experienced!

for him ☆
This sexually creative position will make your partner feel unexpectedly aroused. Your interest may be sustained by your own erotic fantasies.

Arousing a weakened sexual power

The *Kama Sutra* includes some dramatic and commonsense solutions to help men and women experience pleasure together when one or other of them initially fails to become aroused. When writing *The Perfumed Garden,* Sheikh Nefzawi may well have sought inspiration from this text, extracts of which are detailed below.

HER CLIMAX

"If a man is unable to satisfy a *Hastini* (Elephant woman) he should recourse to various means to excite her passion. At the commencement he should rub her *yoni* (vagina) with his hand or fingers, and not begin to have intercourse with her until she becomes excited or experiences pleasure."

ENHANCING THE LINGAM

The *Kama Sutra* advises that a man whose penis is too small should put on an *apadravyas*. This was a sex aid made of materials such as buffalo horn, silver, or copper wire. One form, known as the *Kantuka* or *Jalaka*, was an open-ended tube, outwardly rough and studded with soft globules, that fitted onto the penis and was tied at the waist. Or there was the penis bracelet, made from soft metal with a knobbly surface, which wrapped around the penis.

ERECTION PROBLEMS

Asparagus featured in several recipes to cure men of erection problems. But the solution in which the man plasters the penis with a burning ointment is NOT recommended.

CONTRACTING THE YONI

In the 4th century AD, when the *Kama Sutra* was written, and in the 15th century, when *The Perfumed Garden* was written, most women kept their *yonis* as

A man stimulates his lover's clitoris to pleasure her before intercourse.

small as possible in order to offer the greatest possible friction to their man. The *Kama Sutra* recommends a fruit ointment that apparently kept the *yoni* contracted throughout the night. Another concoction, made by pounding together the roots of several flowers including the blue lotus, was said to enlarge the *yoni*. Tests carried out on Nile lotus flowers in 2001 show that they do, indeed, contain an ingredient responsible for mild sexual arousal.

SERIOUS SADISM

One Brahmin experienced such an extraordinary sexual reaction from being stung by a wasp that his wife insisted his penis be stung over and over again!

Entry from behind
It's not surprising that rear-entry positions feature frequently in our fantasies. The buttocks are thought to generate strong sexual signals, which are heightened during sex, making for spectacular lovemaking.

SIXTH POSTURE

This classic rear-entry position may generate powerfully atavistic feelings in 21st-century lovers. The woman rests on her knees and elbows and parts her legs enough to allow her partner to kneel between them. He holds her around the waist and draws her backward and forward onto his erection. She can lower or heighten her position to match his height by leaning up or down on her elbows and forearms.

for her ☆☆☆

Your man is in a stable enough position for him to have at least one hand free, so ask him to caress your buttocks, back, and breasts and to stimulate your clitoris for maximum arousal.

for him ☆☆☆

This is a naturally pleasurable position for you to thrust deeply and achieve climax as you gaze down at your partner's buttocks and caress her back.

COITUS FROM THE BACK

In this rear-entry position, the man lies flat on top of his partner's back. A pillow is placed underneath the woman's pelvis to raise her hips, so her man can penetrate her deeply and prevent his penis from accidentally slipping out of her vagina.

for him and her☆☆☆

According to Sheikh Nefzawi, this is the easiest of all lovemaking methods. The man's member is aligned with his partner's vagina in such a way as to ensure G-spot stimulation for her and a high level of arousal and deep penetration for both partners.

The womanly ideal

Sheikh Nefzawi desired almost unattainable beauty in his ideal woman. He also looked for compliance and docility—what we in the 21st century would call subservience!

"She speaks and laughs rarely, and never without a reason. She never leaves the house, even to see neighbors of her acquaintance. She has no women friends, gives her confidence to nobody, and her husband is her sole reliance. She takes nothing from anyone, excepting from her husband and her parents. If she sees relatives, she does not meddle with their affairs. She is not treacherous, and has no faults to hide, nor bad reasons to proffer. She does not try to entice people."

Enough said!

Acrobatic positions *Occasionally Sheikh*

Nefzawi described moves that might be better performed at the circus. The positions illustrated over the next few pages do require a certain amount of suppleness, but they also introduce an exciting element of sexual exploration.

SEVENTH POSTURE

The Seventh Posture seems to favor the flexibility only really possessed by gymnasts. Sheikh Nefzawi specifies that the woman lie on her side, although the pose is marginally less difficult if she lies on her back. The man sits back on his heels with one of her legs over his shoulder and the other between his thighs.

Have fun exploring your own personal fantasies as you arouse each other and make love in this face-to-face position.

"Just as all mouths and faces are different, so too are women's vulvas."   *The Perfumed Garden*

THE SEDUCER

This position has two versions. In the first, shown here, the woman wraps her legs around her man's waist to give him leverage as he thrusts. In the second, which provides deeper penetration, she puts her legs over his shoulders.

for him ☆☆☆

Ask your woman to guide your penis into her vagina so she can knead and massage it before insertion. This will give you a little extra stimulation before this sensual position commences.

for her ☆☆

Your man supports your buttocks with his thighs, leaving him at least one free hand to caress your shoulders and breasts. Let him know that the sides of your breasts can be just as sensitive as the nipples, or even more so in some cases.

for him ★☆

At the moment of orgasm, Sheikh Nefzawi suggests that
you grasp your lover's upper arms and draw her to you.

for her ★☆

Enjoy the physical security and intimacy of this position as
you reveal your feelings of vulnerability and trust to your man.

FROG FASHION

This intimate position feels friendly, even though neither partner can move very much. The man holds on to his woman's shoulders and pulls her forward onto his penis. He needs to push her knees back gently so that her heels are close enough to her buttocks to allow him room for entry. She wraps her arms around her knees and leans back. Since her feet are tucked underneath his buttocks, she can lean back with quite a degree of comfort.

Praiseworthy women

Some of the characteristics of Sheikh Nefzawi's ideal woman would be less than attractive to our modern eyes:

"In order that a woman may be relished by men, she must have a perfect waist and be plump and lusty. Her hair will be black, her forehead wide, she will have eyebrows of Ethiopian blackness, large black eyes, with the whites in them very limpid.

"With cheek of perfect oval, she will have an elegant nose and graceful mouth; lips and tongue vermilion; her breath will be of pleasant odor, her throat long, her neck strong; her breasts must be full and firm; the lower part of the belly is to be large, the vulva projecting and fleshy, from the point where the hairs grow, to the buttocks; the conduit must be narrow and not moist, soft to the touch, and emitting a strong heat and no bad smell.

"If one looks at a woman with those qualities in front, one is fascinated; if from behind, one dies with pleasure."

ALTERNATIVE MOVEMENT OF PIERCING

The woman sits between her man's knees so that each lover can place the soles of their feet together. After penetration, he moves her back and forth on his penis instead of thrusting from the pelvis. He can do this by first pulling her toward him and then letting her drop back slightly, or, as Sheikh Nefzawi suggests, she can sit on his feet, which he then moves backward and forward!

for him ☆

You would need to be a strong, flexible athlete with a very small partner if you wanted to achieve this position successfully; perhaps this is one of Nefzawi's personal fantasies that you can translate into your own erotic imaginings.

for her

Your role is an entirely passive one, so watch the pleasure gained by your partner from this position.

The movements of love (from *The Perfumed Garden*)

The Bucket in the Well
"The man and woman join in close embrace after the introduction. Then he gives a push, and withdraws a little; the woman follows him with a push, and also retires. So they continue their alternative movement, keeping proper time. Placing foot against foot and hand against hand, they keep up the motion of a bucket in a well."

The Mutual Shock
"After the introduction, they each draw back, but without dislodging the member completely. Then they both push tightly together, and thus go on keeping time."

The Approach
"The man moves as usual, and then stops. The woman, with the member in her receptacle, moves like the man, then stops. They continue until the ejaculation comes."

EIGHTH POSTURE

To perform the Eighth Posture a woman must be adept at yoga. Perhaps the rewards of this posture are enough to inspire some yoga training! She can lie back in one of two positions: either with her thighs open and her ankles crossed as though performing the lotus position, while her man kneels astride her; or she can cross her legs and pull them back before he enters her, so her legs rest against his chest.

for her ✩✩✩

It makes sense to keep your body in trim to enjoy a strong sexual response. If you practice Kegel exercises (p.36) to strengthen your vaginal muscles, they will contract dramatically during orgasm. Each of the variations of this cross-legged posture has its own benefits. Pull your crossed legs back for deep penetration and G-spot stimulation or cross your ankles for clitoral stimulation. Your lover's hands are free to caress you as you make love, so encourage him to use them as you want.

for him ✩✩✩

To heighten your pleasure, ask your woman to change the position of her hips to vary the angle and depth of your penetration.

The quickie *Spontaneous sex features regularly in our lives in this speedy era. But it doesn't have to be second-best compared to slower, more languid sex. Just the idea of a stolen quickie can be extremely erotic.*

for him and her ☆☆

This profoundly tantalizing position, which can be performed clothed or naked, provides immediate physical satisfaction, as you make the most of a few precious moments.

NINTH POSTURE

This position has three main variants—two rear-entry and one face-to-face. In the rear-entry versions, the woman lies facedown across a bed with her knees on the floor or stands and leans forward over the bed. In the face-to-face version, she lies on her back on a bed with her feet on the floor. All of these positions are easy to get out of should you be interrupted unexpectedly.

Dealing with second and third wives

The *Kama Sutra* and *The Perfumed Garden* were both written at a time when polygamous marriages were considered normal. In some Muslim societies today, it is still common for men to have several wives. Vatsyayana has some fascinating advice for wives in the *Kama Sutra*.

Many of us in the 21st century are in sequential marriages that allow for divorce to pave the way for further relationships and alliances. If children complicate the picture, parents often find that they need to maintain good relations with their previous partners, especially if they spend family occasions together. It's because of this that the following advice from the *Kama Sutra* continues to be relevant today.

BE UNSELFISH
From the very beginning, writes Vatsyayana, a wife should endeavor to attract the heart of her husband by continually showing him her devotion, her good temper, and her wisdom. However, Vatsyayana goes on to say that if a wife does not bear any children, she should take it upon herself to tell her husband to marry again. In this context the gains in medical advancements and IVF are put into a new light.

ACT LIKE AN OLDER SISTER
Vatsyayana notes that when a new wife is married and brought home, the elder wife should give her a position superior to her own and look upon her like a sister. In the morning, the elder wife should make the younger decorate herself in the presence of her husband, and not mind his favors being given to her. "Her children she should treat as her own, her attendants she should look on with more regard even than on her own servants, her friends she should cherish with love and kindness, and her relations

with great honor." But what happened if, despite a younger wife's fecundity, the husband still favored the elder wife? The more wives, the greater the chance of warring factions, rivalry, and jealousy. On the plus side, cowives probably lent each other much support.

IF THERE ARE MANY WIVES
In a harem, the rules changed dramatically. The elder wife "should associate with the one immediately next to her in rank and age, and should instigate the wife who has recently enjoyed her husband's favor to quarrel with his present favorite." Creating strife maintained equality among the wives and evened out the power so that no one could gain complete control.

Wives were expected to tolerate their husband's favorite.

Dominant roles

Positions that are redolent of mild bondage and domination can introduce lovers to the eroticism of helplessness and the power trip of being in control. Contrary to what the uninitiated think, the dominated partner is not as helpless as he or she may seem. These positions could be the perfect way to get your imagination working overtime.

The best wife

Sheikh Nefzawi writes, "If her husband shows his intention of performing the conjugal rite, the wife is agreeable to his desires and occasionally even provokes them. She does not laugh or rejoice when she sees her husband moody or sorrowful, but shares his troubles, and wheedles him into good humor, till he is quite content again. She does not surrender herself to anybody but her husband, even if abstinence would kill her."

TENTH POSTURE

Despite appearances, this is a position in which the woman dominates. She lies with her straight legs parted and her man kneels between her thighs. She then lifts her knees to squeeze her lover around the waist. At the same time she reaches above her head with one or both hands and grasps the headboard. Once he has inserted his penis, the man leans forward to grasp her hands so that the lovers move back and forth with a seesaw motion. Movement for both partners is limited, but since she is in control, her man must respond to her rhythms.

for him and her ☆☆

The action of pulling and pushing against the bed in this way can improve the sensation of your lovemaking by bringing in a sense of urgency that can be thrilling for both of you.

POUNDING ON THE SPOT

This position will feel strangely familiar to any woman used to horseback riding. The movement of her thigh muscles is the same as that used for rising for the trot! The man sits with his legs outstretched, while the woman sits astride him to face him as she guides his penis into her vagina.

for him ☆☆

As you surrender to your partner's movements, your pleasure will increase every time she slides down onto your penis. Ask her to tighten her vaginal muscles to heighten your sexual friction.

for her ☆☆

This position allows you to be incontrol—and power is, after all, an aphrodisiac. Use your vaginal muscles to grip your lover's penis as you move up and down to generate further excitement for yourself.

for him☆☆

This is an interesting
experimental position for any
man who is curious to know
what it feels like to be a woman.
You may enjoy heightened erotic
thoughts as well as physical
sensations in this role-reversal.

for her☆

The advanced position requires
you to have strong legs; you
may not be able to continue
for long, but you will enjoy being
in control and watching your
partner's reactions.

RACE OF THE MEMBER

The man lies with a large cushion under his shoulders and draws his knees up to form a V-shape. The woman faces her lover, lowers herself down between his thighs and inserts his penis into her vagina. In the advanced version, shown here, the man pulls his knees up toward his shoulders so his lover can sit astride his thighs and "ride" him. She needs to push herself up and down on his erect penis by bending her knees. The movement is much like knee bends while skiing—fitness as you frolic!

THE FITTER-IN

What you achieve with the Fitter-In is a living work of art. The woman sits with her legs over her man's thighs. Then, with each taking care to maintain a mutually enjoyable rhythm, the lovers grip each other's arms and rock gently backward and forward. *The Perfumed Garden* recommends that the couple maintain an exact rhythm "by the assistance of their heels which are resting on the ground."

for him ☆☆

A gentle rocking motion rather than a thrusting action provides just enough stimulation to prolong your erection.

for her ☆

This will not be an orgasmic experience for you, but you can enjoy the thought that you are moving in tandem to pleasure each other in such a beautiful coupling that you create a living sculpture.

RECIPROCAL SIGHTS OF THE POSTERIORS

The man lies on his back, ideally with his head propped by a cushion so that he can get a pleasing view of his woman's buttocks as she rises and falls above him. She sits astride her man in any way that pleases her, provided she has her back to him. She can turn her head and body slightly so that she, too, can see her posterior rising and falling. Her balance is best maintained by leaning forward slightly during lovemaking.

for him and her ☆☆

This rather impersonal method of lovemaking allows each partner to have erotic fantasies about enjoying sex with someone else. If they are in a long-term partnership in which desire wanes as familiarity grows, it can be useful to foster such a fantasy, since it may help to reignite the spark of excitement.

Missionary position

Since time immemorial, the classic missionary position has felt good, offered full, body-to-body contact, and allowed couples to kiss and look into each other's eyes as they make love. Perhaps the author of The Perfumed Garden *ends his series of basic poses with this one in recognition of its universal satisfaction!*

ELEVENTH POSTURE

The woman lies on her back to let her lover penetrate her. Her partner leans over her and supports his upper body weight on his hands to begin thrusting. The depth of penetration that is achieved in this position creates intensely pleasurable stimulation for both partners.

for him ★★★★☆

Your greater strength can be used to give you control of your thrusting, and allows you to vary the pace and tempo so that your lovemaking can be long and lingering or rapid and explosive.

for her ★★★☆☆

The Eleventh Posture allows for deep penetration and good clitoral stimulation. The movement of intercourse will pull your labia rhythmically across your clitoris, creating a gentle, stimulating friction that is highly arousing and may trigger orgasm.

THIS HITS THE SPOT

INTERCHANGE
OF COITION

This is the direct opposite of the Eleventh Posture and is another of Sheikh Nefzawi's suggestions for "women acting the part of a man." The man lies on his back with his legs open and a pillow resting between his thighs. For the woman, this is a sophisticated version of a push-up, in which she levers herself up and down while her vagina and thighs tightly grip the man's penis.

for him ★★★

This is an excellent lovemaking position for an older man and his younger partner because it gives the penis the extra stimulation that many older men need in order to increase their ecstasy and reach climax.

for her ★★☆

By varying the angle of thrust slightly, you can ensure that your clitoris is stimulated. Move your pelvis close up against your partner's to enable this to happen. Your only concern in this position is that you are physically strong and fit enough to sustain the movement.

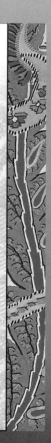

Further movements
of love (from *The Perfumed Garden*)

Love's Tailor
"The man, with his member being only partially inserted, keeps up a sort of quick friction with the part that is in, and then suddenly plunges his member in up to its root."

The Toothpick in the Vulva
"The man introduces his member between the walls of the vulva and then drives it up and down, and right and left. Only a man with a vigorous member can do this."

The Boxing-Up of Love
"The man introduces his member entirely into the vagina, so closely that his hairs are completely mixed up with the woman's. He must now move forcibly, without withdrawing his tool in the least."

Standing positions

Standing up for lovemaking seems to celebrate irrepressible lust and desire. There is a place in every couple's sex life for erotic immediacy, so show the strength of your attraction to each other by being impulsive and abandoned.

BELLY TO BELLY

Each partner stands with their feet firmly on the floor or, if it feels more natural, the woman hooks one leg over her partner's thigh. This enables her to move up and down as they take turns thrusting, using the Bucket in the Well move *(p.104)*. Most of the action comes from her, but the man can help by supporting her in his arms, even lifting her if this feels desirable.

for him and her ✫✫✫

The immediate passion and intensity of your lovemaking will make you both feel blissfully aroused.

DRIVING THE PEG HOME

This position is so named because the movement of the man's penis is akin to that of a peg being driven into a wall. The woman wraps her legs as tightly as possible around the man's waist, holds on to his shoulders, and keeps her back straight against the wall. If he is strong, the man can thrust satisfactorily while lifting his partner at the same time.

for him and her ☆

The man's penis is very vulnerable to damage in this position, so great care must be taken. This is a risky and difficult pose, which could wound or bruise either the man or the woman. It's probably best rated as the kind of sexual activity you might do once for kicks, but in hindsight will confine to that single occasion.

Varying a love life

The worlds of *The Perfumed Garden* and the *Kama Sutra* make it clear that many lovemaking concepts that were considered absolutely fine in those days are now hardly ever included in our own erotic itineraries. However, we can learn from them. Most specifically, we can learn to open our minds when formerly they were closed. If we wouldn't dream of standing sex, for example, maybe we might let go just long enough to give it a try. If we are not turned on by one activity, maybe we can at least let our lover enjoy it. Occasionally in life we learn from giving way to sexual impulses. It's in this way that we learn about our own inner nature.

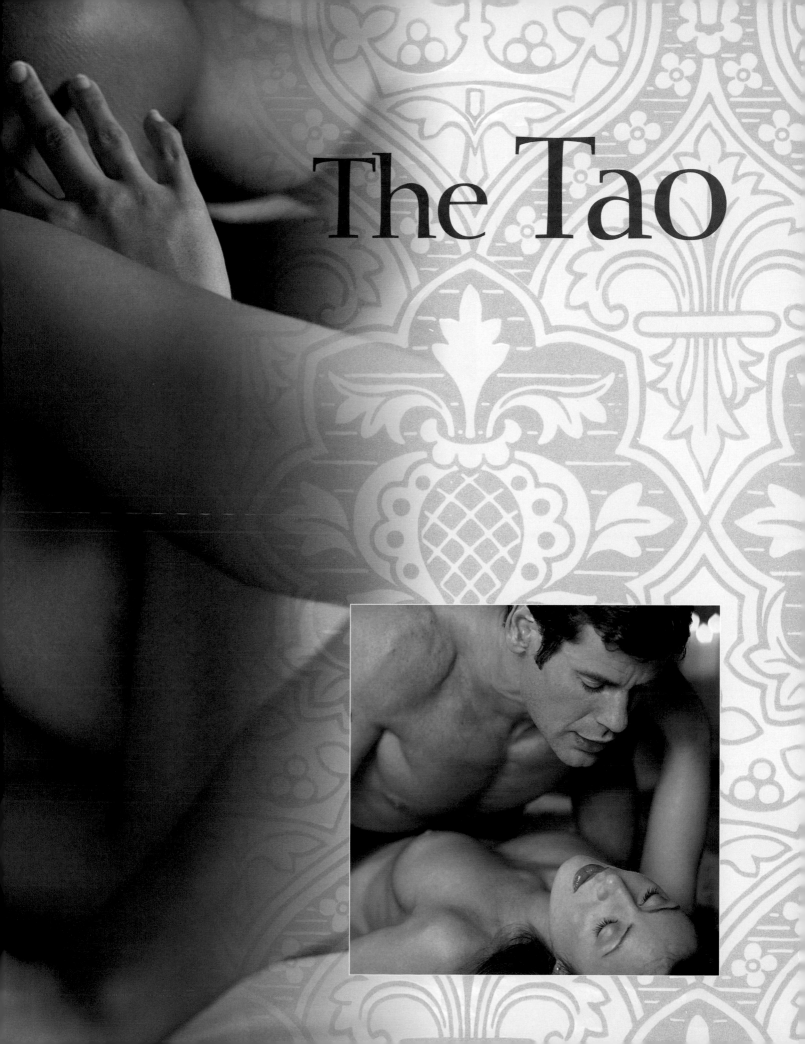

The Tao

Man on top

Tao poses differ from ancient Indian positions in that they are supremely artistic moves; Chinese sex books were choreographed to have a delightful visual appeal. Therefore Tao sex, unlike the kind of sex we enjoy in the 21st century, is to be performed. In The Tao, there are four basic forms of coupling. In the first of these, the man is on top.

DRAGON

The Dragon enables lovers to touch each other in many places and increase their feelings of intimacy. The name derives from the fact that the man, resting on his hands and knees, looks like a dragon. This mythical creature features in the names of several Taoist poses—the dragon being both magical and fiery. The man lies on top of his woman with his legs between hers and his weight on his hands. He inserts his penis against the upper part of her labia and then performs the shallow and deep stroke method of thrusting known as the Sets of Nine *(p.121)*.

for her☆☆☆

According to Yin and Yang philosophy (p.147), this position allows a woman to climax rapidly because of the intimacy it invokes. However, your role in this position is necessarily passive, giving you time to focus on the sensations you feel. If you pride yourself on your active sexual behavior, it can be quite hard to lie back and let go, but for this particular "sexercise" it's worth enjoying the exciting prospect of being fully stimulated to orgasm by your lover.

for him☆☆☆

The tender intimacy of this position, coupled with the tantalizing Sets of Nine you perform, will arouse and excite you.

SWALLOWS IN LOVE

This gentle man-on-top position is inspired by the courtship of birds. The shape that the lovers' bodies make is reminiscent of a swallow with its forked tail. The man lies on top of the woman with his legs between hers and his weight on his elbows. The woman bends her knees slightly to allow him to penetrate her and places her hands around his waist or caresses his body.

for him and her☆☆

Swallows in Love offers only moderate penetration, but gives lovers an opportunity to express their tenderness and enjoy a sense of togetherness. You will each experience a heightening state of arousal in this position.

The Sets of Nine

These are a series of shallow-then-deep penile thrusts performed during intercourse. The theory is that they thoroughly massage the interior of the vagina, giving it sufficient stimulation to allow every energy center in the vagina to come alive.

The sequence goes:

- Nine shallow thrusts
- Eight shallow thrusts and one deep thrust
- Seven shallow thrusts and two deep thrusts
- Six shallow thrusts and three deep thrusts
- Five shallow thrusts and four deep thrusts
- Four shallow thrusts and five deep thrusts
- Three shallow thrusts and six deep thrusts
- Two shallow thrusts and seven deep thrusts
- One shallow thrust and eight deep thrusts
- Nine deep thrusts.

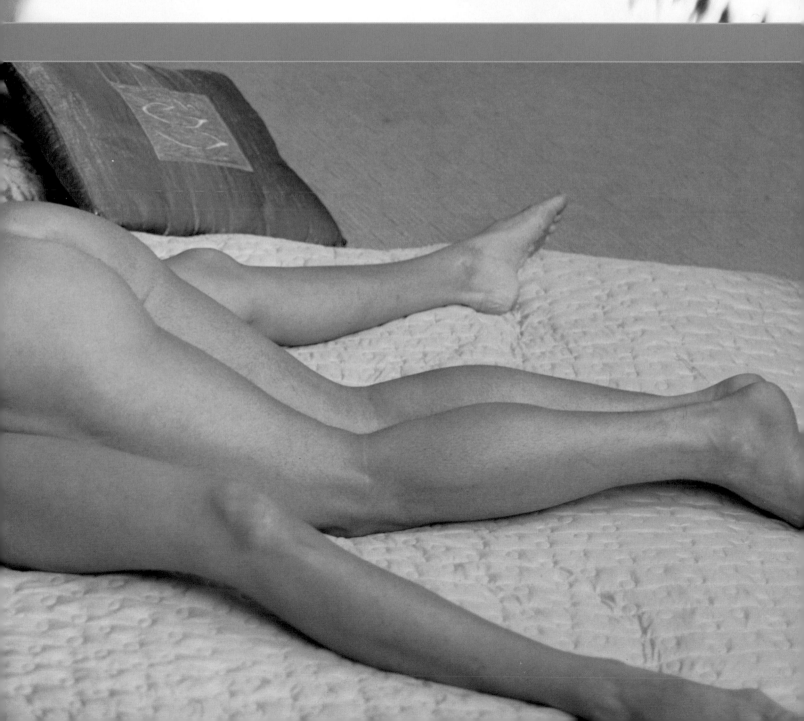

SILKWORM SPINNING A COCOON

The man lies on top of his woman and leans his weight on his hands to support himself so he can use his powerful buttock muscles to thrust. The woman lies beneath him and crosses her ankles behind his back so she can lift and lower her hips in rhythm with his thrusts.

for him ★★★

While you thrust into your partner from this position of power, watch the pleasure and emotions on her face. This will increase your own pleasure and can intensify your orgasm.

for her ★★

Lift and spread your thighs to expose your clitoris to powerful stimulation as you make love. While your lover (the silkworm) is busy spinning, you (the cocoon) can lie back and enjoy some sexual imagery that can contribute to your climax. You may imagine, for instance, that your vagina is a flower and your open legs are the leaves. As you are stimulated, picture the flower opening and blossoming into orgasm.

What is Tao all about?

The central concept of Tao is that there is a system of forces inherent in nature—a natural order—which underpins all life. The goal of the Tao is to live harmoniously with this natural order and master the human condition.

The ancient Chinese believed that the Tao contained eight specific areas over which we must gain mastery to overcome illness and the stresses of life, and obtain harmony with the natural order.

The Tao of Philosophy is a practical and spiritual set of guidelines with which to think through the trickier aspects of life and deal with them effectively and with compassion.

The Tao of Revitalization consists of three systems of internal exercises directed at healing the human body and maintaining it in superb condition.

The first is aimed at correcting posture to balance internal energy (a kind of early Alexander technique).

The second is meditative, aimed at balancing energy flow. The mind, body, and spirit become integrated through meditation techniques and the individual feels energized.

The third is cosmic breathing, in which an individual breathes using techniques that allow the body to absorb energy through its meridian points. Cosmic breathing is also a vital step in self-healing.

The Tao of Balanced Diet focuses on the acid–alkaline balance of foods. Taoist nutrition lists guidelines on the energy levels of food, the five taste sensations, and the nutrient content of food.

The Tao of Forgotten Food Diet is a set of guidelines that highlights the benefits of herbal intake with the aim of healing the body.

The Tao of Healing Art is a form of massage that follows the energy pathways of the body via the meridian points in order to regulate vital functions. Acupuncture is an offshoot of this technique.

A 19th-century Chinese watercolor depicting an erotic Tao position.

The Tao of Sex Wisdom aims to balance the negative with the positive through male and female sexuality, the Yin and the Yang *(see also p.147)*.

The Tao of Mastery provides a set of tools to help us understand people and the world around us:
• *Personology* reveals individuals' abilities and attitudes
• *Fingerprint System* reveals the inherited part of personality and health tendencies
• *Taoist Numerology* offers insight into life patterns
• *Astrology* reveals the likely effects of the solar system on personality
• *Directionology* is a study of the physical laws of nature
• *Symbology* reads symbols indicating natural events.

The Tao of Success explains the mechanics of events and the forces that shape them through a study of symbols representing change (such as branches of mathematics), a study of change and its connotations (written into types of mathematical formulae), and the practice of forecasting events (I-Ching).

HUGE BIRD ABOVE A DARK SEA

In this position, which offers deep penetration, the woman lies on her back with her legs lifted over her partner's arms. The man leans forward against her thighs and raises her buttocks slightly so that they rest against his thighs. He then grasps her around the waist and simultaneously pulls her toward him as he pushes into her.

for him ★★★

By lifting her legs, you change the angle of entry for your penis so that as you thrust, you can penetrate more deeply than in the basic missionary position.

for her ★★★

You may feel very vulnerable, both literally and figuratively, as your legs hang helplessly over your lover's arms. This is a position to try when you are feeling deeply in love with your partner and want to show him your feelings of trust and dependency. You should also feel heightened physical sensations.

GALLOPING HORSE

This position requires the man to hold on to his woman's neck and foot like a bareback rider clinging to a speeding horse. The man kneels between his lover's legs with his thighs beneath her buttocks. She bends her knees to grasp him with her thighs and tucks her feet in close to his. After he has entered her, he holds the back of her neck with one hand, pulls her foot or ankle close to him with the other hand, and begins to thrust.

for him and her ★

The optimum way to make love in this complicated posture is to move up and down, but if the man is tall and the woman is small and light, avoid this position. It could prove to be impossible or dangerous if the man loses his balance. So take care.

PINE TREE

This version of the missionary position allows for deep penetration. The man needs to hold his body clear of his lover's by supporting himself on his hands and knees. The woman can show how eager she is for lovemaking by wrapping her arms and legs passionately around his body.

for him ★★★

This is an ideal position if you have a short penis because it allows you to thrust deeply. If your woman can pull herself up closer to you, she increases the distance that your penis can drive into her vagina and intensifies the sexual tension.

for her ★★☆

By hanging on to your man with your hands and keeping your ankles crossed above his buttocks, you can move in close to increase clitoral stimulation as he penetrates deeper.

> "*The practice of Tao sex is said to keep a woman looking young.*"
>
> *The Tao*

DRAGON TURNS AWAY

…And so too might the lovers, because this position is neither comfortable nor intimate. I would advise that you avoid this position, but it's worth trying once in case it works for you. The woman lies on her back with her legs straight in the air. The man kneels behind her and, using one hand to push her legs as far back as is comfortable for her, he uses the other to guide his penis into her vagina. He should not attempt to enter her until she is fully aroused and her vagina is enlarged to its fullest extent.

for him ☆

Although you can penetrate your partner's vagina deeply while in this position, it is pretty impersonal and unsatisfactory, since any eye contact with her is blocked by her upright legs.

for her

The strain on your legs makes this whole experience unsatisfactory for you, and your clitoris gets virtually no stimulation. Find pleasure in self-stimulation instead!

PHOENIX PLAYING IN A RED CAVE

The imaginative title hints at the possibility of deep penetration in this position—but as with the Dragon Turns Away, the man should wait until the woman is fully aroused before he attempts to insert his penis. The woman lies on her back and holds on to her ankles to expose "the red cave" in which her kneeling lover's penis wants to "play."

for her ☆☆

This position may prove tiring for you if sustained for too long, so enjoy the arousal and stimulation your partner gives you before penetration. He can encourage you by rubbing his penis up and down your inner labia, then across or around your clitoris.

for him ☆☆

Once your partner is fully aroused, enjoy the sexual friction of intercourse and the urge to control the action as you thrust rhythmically.

The Taoist pillow books

The ancient Chinese read sex manuals, known as pillow books, to understand not only the mechanics of sex, but how best to acquire uninhibited sexual expression as part of living a long and full life. The best known of the Taoist pillow books is the *T'ung Hsuan Tzu*, written by the 7th-century physician Li T'ung Hsuan. Even today, such candid writings and explicit, yet beautiful, illustrations can appear pornographic to Western eyes.

However, the pillow books excluded any reference to homosexual and lesbian practices, justified by the Taoist principle that true sexual union is the interplay of equal and opposite forces embodied by men and women—a view no longer in keeping with this day and age.

MANDARIN DUCK

Mandarin ducks mate for life and so are considered lovebirds and symbols of marriage in China. The woman lies on her back with her right leg stretched out. Then, leaning over slightly to the right, she bends her left knee and raises her leg. The man faces her and sits on top of her thighs. He rests his weight on his left leg by kneeling on the bed or squatting (if he has strong legs). He then bends his right knee and moves his right leg forward under his lover's raised left leg. As he does this, he also penetrates her. His weight rests slightly on her thighs, and there is something ducklike about his intent squat.

for him and her☆☆

You may find yourselves tuning in to and heightening each other's passion in this creative position. However, the man may find it difficult to maintain his balance for very long.

SEAGULLS ON THE WING

Perhaps the woman's wide-open knees symbolize a seagull's wings. She lies with her buttocks on the edge of the bed, her feet on the ground to support her and her legs apart. The man kneels up against the side of the bed between his lover's knees and pulls her toward him just enough to make penetration easy.

for him and her☆☆☆☆

In most man-on-top positions, the man's penis thrusts downward into the vagina, but here the penis and vagina are parallel, so for both partners the sensations feel very different and extremely exciting. There is certainly something very abandoned in the way the woman slips halfway off the bed as her lover thrusts wildly.

HORSE CROSS FEET

There are distinct undertones of bondage here in the way the man grasps his lover's ankles and locks her leg into position. The animal symbolism refers to the image of a horse's legs appearing to cross over as it gallops, and the visual mixture of the woman's hand and knee do indeed give such an impression. The woman lies on her back and bends her left knee while the man kneels in front of her and leans over her. He steadies himself by placing his left hand by her right shoulder and putting his weight on it. He clasps her left ankle with his right hand and, drawing her close, penetrates her. He then thrusts fast to gain the sensation of galloping.

for him☆☆
This is a tiring but exciting position that opens you up to deeper sensation later on.

for her☆☆
If you wish, clasp your man's right hand so that you rock in time with his "galloping." Some women find this easier if both legs are bent instead of just one.

DRAGON TURN

To the ancient Chinese, the long limbs and flexible bodies displayed in this position resembled the mythical dragon. The woman's knees and elbows do, indeed, convey the impression of dragon wings. She lies on her back with her legs bent at the knees. Her hands hold her knees wide apart, and she lifts her feet up high so that her heels rest on her man's hips as he kneels on either side of her buttocks. He supports himself on his hands so that he can penetrate his partner and begin deep and shallow thrusts, as in the Sets of Nine *(p.121)*.

for him ☆☆☆☆

Pressing down onto your woman allows you to have more control over your thrusting so that you can explore and experiment with erotically intense lovemaking skills.

for her ☆☆☆☆

As your lover performs his Sets of Nine, his penis touches different parts of your vagina. With your legs in this position, you can have deeply pleasurable sensations and increased feelings of ecstasy.

"Woman's orgasm is a series of eight upward rising steps, then one declining."

The Tao

Language of The Tao

The writers of the many Taoist pillow books, like their Indian and Arab counterparts, took much inspiration from nature when describing sexual matters in their typically poetic style:

The Male Sexual Organ
Jade, Stem, Coral Stem, Male Stalk, Turtle Head, Red Bird, Heavenly Dragon Pillar

The Female Sexual Organ
Coral Gate, Jade Gate, Cinnabar Gate, Vermilion Gate, Jade Pavilion, Golden Lotus, Open Peony Blossom, Receptive Vase, Pearl on the Jade Step (clitoris), Jewel Terrace (clitoral area)

Orgasm
The Great Typhoon, Bursting of the Clouds

Sexual Union
The Mists and the Rain, The Clouds and the Rain, The Delight of the Couch.

Woman on top
Since the Taoist goal is to maximize vaginal stimulation (effectively through internal massage by the penis), these woman-on-top positions make sense because they allow the woman to control what happens during thrusting.

BUTTERFLIES IN FLIGHT

The movements of the woman's outstretched arms, or wings, in this evocative position are perhaps like those of a fluttering butterfly. The woman lies on top of her lover, and once she has lowered herself onto his penis, both partners stretch their arms out to either side and hold hands.

CAT AND MICE SHARING A HOLE

This is a straightforward love position in which the woman lies full-length along her partner's body with her knees on either side of his thighs and her hands supporting her weight.

for him and her☆☆☆

Although strenuous effort is required if either partner is to reach orgasm like this, your striving together can be mutually exciting. However, considering its evocative title, I find this a disappointing version of the love position. My own choice would include active stimulation by the hands and fingers, which can stand in as "mice." Since the man has both hands free, he can caress his lover's buttocks and back, and also her breasts and clitoris.

for him☆☆☆

Your movement is very limited unless your partner is light, but this is an extremely pleasurable position when you are tired or when your woman wants to assume the male's role and make love to you.

for her☆☆☆

Push your toes against your man's feet to move up and down and increase the sexual friction. This will provide thrilling sensations as his penis moves inside your vagina.

BIRDS FLY BACK ON BACK

This position can be interpreted as two mating birds in flight. It takes quite a stretch of imagination to see it, but the poetic name makes it an intriguing pose to try. The man lies on his back, and the woman, with her back to her lover, lowers herself into a sitting position on to him and carefully inserts his penis into her vagina. She then drops her head and leans forward slightly. The idea is that she positions her weight over her feet, grasps her ankles or knees, and raises and lowers herself on his penis using her thigh muscles.

for him ☆☆☆
Watching your woman's moving buttocks as she makes love to you may bring you to a state of high arousal. Be careful not to let your penis slip partially from her vagina as you may incur a painful injury.

for her ☆☆☆
You may enjoy your dominant role in awakening your partner's desire. This is a tiring position, but your partner can aid your momentum if he grasps your hips and helps you to move up and down.

BUTTERFLY

This position resembles a butterfly not so much in its shape as in the woman's movements. She sits on her lover's hips, inserts his penis into her vagina, and leans back on her hands, which she places on his legs. She then uses her legs to raise her hips slowly up and down on his penis. It is the movement of her body, with her knees jutting high, that resembles a butterfly in flight.

for him and her ✩✩✩

This role-reversal position may serve to heighten each partner's erotic desires and sexual passions. As in the position shown opposite, if the woman needs help with her movements, the man can reach forward to hold her hips and help her rise and fall.

Injaculation

If we consider Taoist philosophy, the male orgasm could be described as "going" rather than "coming." This is because everything—erection, sperm, nutrients—leaves the body. Taoists believe that by moving energy down through the body and away during ejaculation, you progress in a natural direction. Every living thing starts life filled with energy or "life essence" that gradually drains away, leading ultimately to death. If you can move your energy in the opposite direction, you may prolong your life or even become immortal! This is the aim of Tao sex techniques such as injaculation, which allows the man to experience the pleasure of climax without ejaculating. By pressing the Jen-Mo meridian point, sited between the anus and scrotum, the man can block his seminal tube and retain his "life essence."

A SINGING MONKEY

In this position the woman sits in her lover's lap and curls herself around him as if she were a monkey clinging to him. Although each lover is quite restricted in their movements, they can caress each other's bodies and make eye contact, creating an intimate tenderness between them. The woman leans back on her outstretched hand to lever her pelvis up and down in a type of thrusting motion.

for her ☆☆☆

If you wish, ask your man to place his hand beneath your buttocks. This subtle addition makes for a major turn-on. Many women find this action especially arousing. He can also stretch your buttocks slightly to the side, increasing pressure on the perineum to generate exciting sensations.

for him ☆☆

You have little opportunity to move in this position, so enjoy the feelings of intimacy and emotional contact as your woman makes love to you.

FISH

This pose is so named because the woman's movements look like the flick of a fish's tail as it darts through the water. The man lies on his back with his legs extended and she lies on top of him. She moves forward a little and takes in the tip of her man's penis with her labia. Slowly she wiggles his penis inside her vagina (it may need manual help here). Once she has enclosed him, she moves her hips to the right and left, and up and down, in a repeated sequence.

for him ☆☆

In this passive position you can enjoy the movement of your lover's breasts against your chest as she moves sensuously to pleasure you.

for her ☆

This position is a tantalizingly slow, sensual way to excite you as well as your partner, and leaves you very much in control of the lovemaking.

Sweet-smelling skin

We all of us smell, although our body odor is not necessarily unpleasant. In the best circumstances, it's a pure aphrodisiac. The strength of body scent depends largely on diet. If you eat heavily spiced foods, you will smell of these elements. If you change to vegetarian, unspiced, or herbal diets, the body odor changes to become sweet. This is because vegetables and herbs cleanse the body of its toxins and leave it sweet-smelling. So, too, will regular bathing. Men should practice penile hygiene, ensuring that, if they have a foreskin, they wash regularly underneath it. Men and women also need to ensure that their dental care is meticulous. This may all sound laughably basic, but smell alone can be enough to put you off or turn you on!

Rear entry

The primal appeal of rear-entry positions can be erotically exciting to both sexes. Buttocks inspire an atavistic urge that rear entry can satisfy, but such positions are also perfect for those explosive times when you both want to indulge in fantasy. On such occasions, rear entry is not as distracting as face-to-face sex.

CICADA ON A BOUGH

This is a classic rear-entry position in which the woman lies on her front and the man stretches out along her body with his knees between hers. He pushes his toes against the bed as he thrusts. The shape the two bodies make does, indeed, look like a cicada perched on a branch. The man should try not to put too much weight on his (usually smaller) partner's body and crush her.

for him ☆☆☆☆

It may help to place a pillow under your lover's hips. This allows you deeper penetration, increasing your feelings of ecstasy.

for her ☆☆☆

This exciting position is not guaranteed to give you much stimulation, since your clitoris will be wedged against the bed or the cushion. You can ask your partner to position a vibrator strategically beneath your clitoris so that each time he thrusts, your pelvis pushes down on to the vibrator and together you experience a mutually ecstatic rhythm.

THIS HITS THE SPOT

APE

This position is traditionally favored by Chinese men because it offers them a titillating view of their partner's labia. As the woman lies on her back, raises her legs up high, and rests them on her partner's shoulders, the man kneels to lift her up gently by the hips and draw her sensitively onto his penis. He makes shallow thrusts to begin with, but gradually, as the vagina becomes moister, his thrusting can grow deeper and stronger. The Sets of Nine *(p.121)* works well for this situation.

for him ★★★★☆

The accessibility of your lover's vagina means that you do not have to support your own weight. That makes this an ideal position for the older or heavier man.

for her ☆

Thanks to your pelvic area being relatively unimpeded, you have easy access to your own clitoris should you wish to use your fingers to bring yourself to orgasm.

PINE TREE

This is another position in which the woman lies on her back with her legs raised and resting on her partner's shoulders. The shape of her straight legs is thought to resemble a straight-growing pine tree. She holds her kneeling partner around the hips while he places his hands around her waist and then penetrates her.

for him and her☆☆☆☆

Unlike in many positions, where thrusting is left up to the intensity of desire of that moment, the man's thrusts should be hard and fast. Because of this, the position may provide you both with a more intense physical experience than most poses.

TURTLE MOVE

The languid dog-paddle motion of a turtle afloat in tropical seas can be mimicked by the twin movements of penetration and withdrawal in this position. The woman lies on her back with her legs raised while the man kneels up, holds on to her uplifted thighs, and thrusts into her with slow and deliberate moves. He should pull his penis out almost entirely before starting each following stroke. As her man does this, the woman pulls back from his penis, feeling the long withdrawal that he makes, then pushes forward as he slowly penetrates her again.

for him and her☆☆☆

The slow, deliberate movements of your lovemaking while the man holds the woman tightly will excite you both, and the resistance of your bodies against each other will take you both to orgasm easily.

for him ☆☆

This is another good position for older men who get tired quickly by performing man-on-top positions. It does, however, require that your partner is quite flexible. She may have one hand free to caress your body and heighten your senses as you make love.

for her ☆

At this angle, your partner penetrates you deeply, which increases the erotic tension you feel.

HORSE SHAKES FEET

The Chinese consider this a playful sex position. If the woman shakes the foot of her bent leg during penetration it gives an extra frisson to the lovemaking, but she must be careful not to knock her man over—or even out! The woman lies on her back and places one foot up over her partner's shoulder. She draws back the other leg close to her body so her knee is by her shoulder. If it feels comfortable, her foot can rest on her man's chest while he moves. The man, kneeling upright, penetrates his woman and thrusts deeply.

JADE JOINT

The process of carving and joining together two pieces of jade to form a jade joint, or jade cross, is considered an art form in China. To replicate this revered pattern, the woman lies on her right side and bends her left leg at the knee, pulling it up to hip-level with her left hand. The man kneels behind his woman's hips, holds her left leg up and across him, and penetrates her deeply.

for her☆☆☆

By pulling your leg back, you stretch the vaginal area, which makes you feel exposed, vulnerable and sensuous. This will be an erotic turn-on for you both.

for him☆☆

The deep penetration and sexual friction you can achieve in this position will heighten your excitement and pleasure.

TIGER STEP

Many women find it difficult to remain upright during vigorous thrusting. One method of overcoming this feeling of instability can be to adopt a posture in which the woman rests her forearms and head on the ground. In Tiger Step, she begins in the same kneeling position as in the White Tiger, then lowers her forearms and head to the ground so her body is buttressed against her lover's vigorous thrusts as he kneels behind her.

for him ✰✰✰

Depending on your stamina, you need to thrust as quickly and as deeply as you can until you reach orgasm.

for her ✰

Since you support yourself in this position, your man does not have to hold up his body weight in the same way as for the White Tiger. This leaves his hands free to roam across your back, enlivening you with his touch and increasing your levels of arousal.

WHITE TIGER

The woman's kneeling form in White Tiger is thought to be reminiscent of the shape a tigress makes during congress. This rear-entry position calls for the man to kneel as he thrusts into his woman from behind. He can draw her to him by placing his hands on her waist. The woman raises or lowers her body to suit her partner's height by using her arms to adjust the angle of her torso.

for him ✰✰✰

Watching your woman's buttocks move as you thrust into her is an erotic advantage of this position.

for her ✰✰✰

Encourage your partner to stimulate your clitoris by reaching around in front of your thighs and stroking you as he thrusts.

The Deer Exercise for women

The Deer Exercise is thought to strengthen the female system, balance the hormones, stave off signs of aging, and energize the glands to bring harmony and health. It consists of two stages of exercises that are to be carried out regularly every day.

Stage One Sit with the heel of the foot pressed up against the vagina to give a firm pressure on the clitoris. Rub your hands together vigorously to make

them hot. Rub your breasts in slow, outward, circular motions for a minimum of 36 times and a maximum of 360 times, twice a day.

Stage Two The following exercise can be done either sitting or lying down. Flex the vaginal muscles in a fashion similar to the Kegel exercises (p.36). As you do, press and rub the labia in a type of massage. Your man can assist with one or all of these exercises if you wish.

for him and her ☆

Feel free to explore each other's bodies and awaken your erotic senses in more ways than one. And as each movement heightens your desire, before you know it, the man may be snacking on his woman's tasty body! Either the woman or the man may stimulate the woman's clitoris with their fingers to help her to climax. The spontaneity of this intimate position will excite and pleasure you both.

THE GOAT AND THE TREE

This is the sort of playful game that could develop from a couple's casually playing around together as the woman sits on her man's knee during a conversation or to initiate kissing. It represents a hungry goat nibbling at a delicious tree. The woman sits astride her man with her feet on the floor so that she can rock gently backward and forward on his penis. Although the man's movements are restricted, his hands are free to roam around his partner's body, stroking and caressing her— preferably in some choice erotic spots—as he nibbles on her shoulder.

The pleasures of Yin–Yang sex

The Taoist philosophy of sex is rooted in the principle of Yin and Yang—the universal balance of negative and positive. This harmony is manifested in sex as the active, penetrating penis of the male (Yang) stimulates the absorbing, recessive vagina of the female (Yin).

The positive blending of Yin and Yang energies in a marriage creates a harmonizing resonance. Both partners are responsible for attaining balance within themselves *(see also p.123)*. This takes the form of embodying virtues, even within the sexual organs.

THE FIVE VIRTUES OF THE PENIS

To balance the male body, the penis must be massaged, preferably through intercourse. Taoists believe the penis symbolizes God because it is completely Yang and giving and possesses five virtues.

Kindness The erect penis is kind to women because it gives them pleasure over and over again.

Righteousness The penis is capable of giving without thought for itself.

Courteousness The penis pleases whenever it can. It will be hard and soft at the optimum moments, and its shape, being curved, will not hurt anyone.

Wisdom It learns ways of pleasuring women and will do the best it can to satisfy.

Honesty The erect penis keeps going for as long as it takes to pleasure a woman. And if it just can't manage, it gives up entirely. This makes it totally honest.

THE NINE LEVELS OF ORGASM IN WOMEN

Taoists believe that a woman who can experience a thorough orgasm will achieve physical balance. Modern sex therapy decrees that orgasm has three or four levels. According to Tao sexology, it has up to nine. (All nine levels have a corresponding effect on one or more of the body's major organs.) The first four levels consist of sighing, breathing heavily, grasping and holding, then a series of vaginal spasms that are wrongly considered to be the end of the matter. If a man continues to stimulate his lover beyond these, she can go on to further levels.

Five The woman loosens up throughout her body and she begins to bite at the man.

Six She undulates and writhes with pleasure.

Seven She is boiling hot and tries to touch her man everywhere.

Eight Suddenly her muscles totally relax.

Nine She collapses in a "little death," sighing and moaning.

A Chinese woman massages her lover's penis before intercourse.

LATE SPRING DONKEY

This position is so named because it mimics the mating behavior of donkeys in springtime. The woman bends over at the waist and, keeping her legs as straight as she can, places both hands on the floor. Holding the woman around the waist, the man pulls her toward his erect penis. This is a playful move to be enjoyed as a game and not to be taken too seriously!

for him☆☆☆

Your grip on your woman's waist allows you to thrust without losing your balance and helps you to control the depth of penetration for heightened enjoyment. Ensure that she is fully aroused before you penetrate her.

for her☆

This is not a position most women would want to adopt for any length of time. After a few moments with your head pointing toward the floor, you get a rush of blood to the brain, your breathing becomes constricted, and your perception of the sexual activity changes. If you can climax this way, your orgasm could be considerably enhanced, but you are just as likely to end up with a crushing headache!

RABBIT GROOMING

This hunched-over position is perhaps reminiscent of a rabbit grooming itself. The man lies on his back while the woman sits on top of him, facing toward his feet. Her knees are bent as she leans forward slightly and keeps her hands on the ground. As she encloses her man, she moves her hips in a circular motion—a little like hula-hooping.

for him ☆☆☆

Your partner must judge the force of her sideways movements, since a sudden, awkward thrust might dislodge and hurt your penis. Help your woman control her movements and sustain your erection by keeping your hands on her waist.

for her ☆☆☆

Some women find Rabbit Grooming difficult at first because it requires flexible knee joints and strong leg muscles. But it's worth pursuing, because the circular movement of your hips creates many unusual and wonderful sensations.

Full-body intimacy
For lovers who adore a touch of romance, these lovemaking positions are ideal. They allow a couple to absorb themselves in each other's bodies and experience all-over touch. Expanses of naked skin will tingle as bodies rub together while lovers kiss and caress. Since they are face-to-face, they can see each other's responses, which serves to increase their sexual and emotional intensity.

CICADA TO THE SIDE

This position is similar to Cicada on a Bough *(pp.138–39)* but with the added twist that, although the lovers face one another, their bodies are snuggled into the spoons position. The woman lies on her side while the man presses up against her back and penetrates her gently from the rear, keeping his movements shallow. With his right hand he can turn her chest and head so they can kiss and whisper to each other.

for him and her ☆☆

This is a perfect position for slow, affectionate lovemaking when the woman is heavily pregnant, or for those sexy moments first thing in the morning when you are only half-conscious. Your sleepy desire will develop gradually into an energizing sexual heat of passion and orgasm.

MANDARIN DUCKS

As with the man-on-top version of Mandarin Duck *(p.128)*, this rear-entry version invokes faithful affection as lovers turn their heads adoringly toward each other. It is similar to Cicada to the Side *(pp.150–51)*, in which the woman lies on her side with her man pressed against her back, except that here the man lifts his head to gaze at his lover while she lies drowsily beside him.

for him and her☆☆☆

There is a delightfully sensual and seductive aspect to the man unexpectedly making love to his woman from the rear, especially if you are both just waking up. This position allows him to thrust easily, and by keeping her thighs together the woman can increase the pleasurable friction created by his penis inside her.

TWO FISHES

The arrangement of lovers' legs in this position resembles two fish bending their tails around each other's bodies as they mate. The couple lies side-by-side facing each other, with their legs stretched out. After penetration, the man lifts the woman's legs (which she holds together) and places them on top of his own. The lovers then undulate together rhythmically until they climax.

for him and her ✩✩

This is a good position for shallow, sensitive strokes. The man can alter the angle of the penis in the vagina by moving his lover's legs slightly to vary the sensations. For this kind of front-on, side-by-side intercourse to work well, the man needs quite a long penis: due to the position of the woman's legs, only a short part of the penis can slip inside the vagina, and it may easily slip out again.

To experience life is to experience God

Unfortunately, many people think that sex is a dirty thing because of the repressive ethics they have been brought up with. Taoism has a much more positive view of human sexuality. It embraces human spiritual development through a physical pathway, and advocates that sexual instincts serve this purpose. Taoist sex techniques provide couples with direct, tangible tools to use on this divine path.

All aspects of love in the physical sense—the sharing and the giving—enable men and women to experience God. Tao techniques allow couples to tap into their own bodily electricity and to merge this energy by the thorough mingling of the sexual organs during intercourse. Energy given off by good sex offers not just physical release, but also spiritual recognition. Loving sex can therefore be a religious experience.

BAMBOO

Not all face-to-face love positions involve lying down. In Bamboo, we find a direct and lustful standing posture, with the upright bodies of the lovers resembling two bamboo stalks. The man stands facing his woman and holds her around the waist to penetrate her. She steadies herself by leaning back on her hands, which she places on a bed or table behind her. The logical conclusion is that, as the atmosphere heats up, the couple collapses and the bamboo stalks come crashing down!

for him ★★★

As your desire increases, caress and kiss your lover's body and mouth, or embrace her with your arms and let your hands roam across her back. If your partner is shorter than you in height, or if you have a long penis, you should bend your knees if necessary so that you can fit inside her.

for her ★★★

The angle of your man's penis will stimulate the front of your vagina and give you wonderful sensations.

Sex as a joke

This gravity-defying position is humorous enough to try for fun.

AUTUMN DOG

Size really does matter in this crazy position. It would only be possible if attempted by a man with a long or curved penis. It gets its name from the inelegant mountings of dogs that spurn sexual grace in their rush to get on with things. The man and woman each bend over so their buttocks are touching. Her feet need to be propped up as high as possible to give her man a sporting change of success. The idea is that somehow he penetrates her to perform shallow thrusts.

for him and her

This position may prove too difficult for many of us to achieve successfully, but so what? You can collapse into giggles together as you try!

The Deer Exercise for men

This exercise was believed to rejuvenate men by building up sexual tissue, drawing up energy into the Seven Glands of the body, increasing blood circulation to the abdomen, and generally balancing the sexual system.

Stage One Rub the palms of your hands together to generate warmth. With your right hand, cup the testicles and place the palm of the left hand on your pubis. With a slight pressure, move your left hand (on the pubis) in circles, 81 times. Then rub your hands together again vigorously for warmth and reverse the position of the hands, doing the exercise now with the right hand. Concentrate on what you are doing and let the warmth grow.

Stage Two Contract and release your rectal muscles regularly, morning and evening.

Safer sex

Although there is no mention made of disease that is transmitted through sex in the *Kama Sutra*, we know that people have sought to avoid these infections throughout history. The practice of "safe sex," prompted by the dramatic spread of AIDS (Acquired Immune Deficiency Syndrome) since the 1980s, aims to limit exposure to infection by HIV (Human Immunodeficiency Virus, which causes AIDS) as well as other sexually transmitted infections.

HIV can be carried in bodily fluids—semen, vaginal fluids, and blood—and passed from one person to another during sex. The most effective way of minimizing the exchange of bodily fluids (therefore reducing the risk of transmitting sexually transmitted infections during intercourse) is to use a latex condom with a spermicide, which kills sperm.

HOW TO USE A CONDOM SAFELY

The process of slipping a condom onto your lover's penis can become a natural part of a woman's sensual, erotic lovemaking. Give your lover a genital massage until he has an erection. Then remove the condom carefully from its foil packet, squeeze out the air by holding the top between

thumb and forefinger (a trapped bubble could cause it to split during intercourse), and use slow, sensuous hand movements to roll it down over his penis. Try to make the rolling on of the condom part of your sensual massage. If your lover is not circumcised, gently push back his foreskin before unrolling the condom.

After ejaculation, the man needs to hold the condom on his penis by grasping it around the base of the penis and withdrawing from his woman before his erection subsides. This prevents spillage from the condom.

Some men dislike using condoms on the grounds that it anesthetizes their penis and prevents them from enjoying full sensation during lovemaking. In these situations, the woman might choose to use a female condom, which she can insert into her vagina to serve the same protective purpose as a man's condom.

Non-penetrative sex

There are a few risks attached to non-penetrative sex, although significantly fewer than those attached to intercourse. Dry kissing, embracing, stroking, and massage all express affection and love eloquently, with minimal HIV risk. However, each partner should ensure that no semen or vaginal fluid comes into contact with any cuts, abrasions, or open sores on their fingers or hands if they embark on mutual masturbation.

Oral sex is a high-risk activity, particularly if the bodily fluids it produces are swallowed. A degree of protection can be provided if you use a condom during fellatio and a latex barrier (dental dam) during cunnilingus, although neither method is totally safe.

Index

Acknowledgments

Publisher's Acknowledgments
Dorling Kindersley would like to thank Carla De Abreu
for design support, Laurence Errington for the index and
Alyson Lacewing for proofreading.

Photographer: Russel Kientsch, assisted by Charlie
Pritchard Williams.

Models: Donna-Louise Bryan, Glen Davis, James Davis,
Amanda Llewellyn-Dawkins, Raja Farrar, Jules Haughton,
Lee Henshaw, Billie Howell, Leon James, Jasmine, Katie Lawrie,
Nathan Long, Lucy-Zara McKeown, Mark Stocks, Abigail
Toyne, and Natasha Vale.

Hair and makeup artist: Clare Bonser.

Stylist: Melanie Coles.

Set Builders: Set to Set.

Props kindly supplied by: The Pier, Jali Ltd, CP. Hart, Next
Home, Bath House, and Descamps.

Illustrator: Max Schindler.

Picture researcher: Anna Bedewell.

Dorling Kindersley would like to thank the following for
their kind permission to reproduce their photographs:
(Abbreviations key: t=top, b=bottom, r=right, l=left, c=center)

Endpapers: Robert Harding Picture Library; **3:** Elizabeth Whiting
& Associates (r); **5:** Elizabeth Whiting & Associates (r); **6:** AKG
London: Erich Lessing (l), Werner Forman Archive: (bl); **7:** AKG
London: Erich Lessing (l), © Christie's Images Ltd (tl), Courtesy
of the Trustees of the V&A Picture Library (bl); **8:** AKG London:
Erich Lessing (l), Bridgeman Art Library, London / New York (cl);
9: AKG London: Erich Lessing (l), Bridgeman Art Library,
London / New York (cl); **11:** Elizabeth Whiting & Associates (r);
15: Elizabeth Whiting & Associates (bl), (bc); **16:** Elizabeth
Whiting & Associates (tl), (tc); **20:** Elizabeth Whiting & Associates
(tr), (tc); **21:** Elizabeth Whiting & Associates (tc), (tr);
22: Elizabeth Whiting & Associates (br), (b); **25:** Elizabeth
Whiting & Associates (br), (b); **27:** Elizabeth Whiting & Associates
(r); **32:** Getty Images: Vera Storman (t); **33:** Bridgeman Art
Library, London / New York (cr), Getty Images: Vera Storman (t),
Elizabeth Whiting & Associates (c); **34:** Bridgeman Art Library,
London / New York (tr), Elizabeth Whiting & Associates (tr);
35: AKG London: Jean-Louis Nou (c), (br); **35:** Courtesy of the
Trustees of the V&A Picture Library (r); **36:** Bridgeman Art
Library, London / New York (tr), Elizabeth Whiting & Associates
(t); **45:** © Christie's Images Ltd (cr), Courtesy of the Trustees of
the V&A Picture Library (r); **49:** Getty Images: Vera Storman (r);

51: Bridgeman Art Library, London / New York (tr), Elizabeth
Whiting & Associates (tr); **57:** © Christie's Images Ltd (r);
60: AKG London: Erich Lessing (tr); **61:** AKG London (br),
© Christie's Images Ltd (r); **65:** Getty Images: Vera R Storman (r);
66: AKG London: Erich Lessing (br), © Christie's Images
Ltd (b); **69:** AKG London: Erich Lessing (tr), © Christie's
Images Ltd (t); **71:** AKG London: Erich Lessing (br), © Christie's
Images Ltd (b); **73:** Getty Images: Vera R Storman (tr), (br);
75: AKG London: Erich Lessing (br), © Christie's Images Ltd (b);
78: © Christie's Images Ltd (tc); **79:** Bridgeman Art Library,
London / New York: Fitzwilliam Museum, University of
Cambridge, UK (cr), Musée Guimet, Paris, France (bl); **83:** Link
Image (r); **87:** Photonica: Masano Kawana (r); **89:** Bridgeman
Art Library, London / New York: The Design Library, New York
(tr), Link Image (tc); **91:** Bridgeman Art Library, London / New
York: The Design Library, New York (tr), Link Image (tc);
95: Bridgeman Art Library, London / New York: The Design
Library, New York (br), Link Image (bc); **97:** Bridgeman Art
Library, London / New York (cr), Link Image (r); **99:** Bridgeman
Art Library, London / New York: The Design Library, New York
(tr), Link Image (tc); **103:** Photonica: Masano Kawana (r);
104: Bridgeman Art Library, London / New York: The Design
Library, New York (br), Link Image (b); **107:** © Christie's Images
Ltd (br), Link Image (r); **108:** Bridgeman Art Library, London /
New York: The Design Library, New York (tr), Link Image (tc);
113: Bridgeman Art Library, London / New York: The Design
Library, New York (cr), Link Image (c); **115:** Bridgeman Art
Library, London / New York: The Design Library, New York
(bc), Link Image (bl); **117:** Elizabeth Whiting & Associates (r);
120: Getty Images: Miguel S Salmeron; **121:** Getty Images:
Miguel S Salmeron (t); **123:** Bridgeman Art Library, London /
New York; **127:** Bridgeman Art Library, London / New York (br),
Elizabeth Whiting & Associates (bc); **131:** Bridgeman Art
Library, London / New York (br), Elizabeth Whiting & Associates
(bc); **135:** Bridgeman Art Library, London / New York (tr),
Elizabeth Whiting & Associates (tc); **137:** Bridgeman Art
Library, London / New York (bc), Elizabeth Whiting &
Associates (bl); **144:** Bridgeman Art Library, London / New
York (br), Elizabeth Whiting & Associates (b); **147:** Bridgeman
Art Library, London / New York (br), Elizabeth Whiting &
Associates (r); **153:** Bridgeman Art Library, London / New
York (tr), Elizabeth Whiting & Associates (tc); **155:** Bridgeman
Art Library, London / New York (tr), Elizabeth Whiting &
Associates (tc); **157:** Elizabeth Whiting & Associates (tc), (tr);
158, 159, 160: Elizabeth Whiting & Associates.

All other images © Dorling Kindersley Limited.
For further information see: www.dkimages.com.